A Modern Pilgrimage in New Testament Christology

NORMAN PERRIN

A Modern Pilgrimage in New Testament Christology

FORTRESS PRESS
Philadelphia

COPYRIGHT © 1974 BY FORTRESS PRESS

Library of Congress Catalog Card Number 73-88352

ISBN 0-8006-0267-6

4021H73   Printed in U.S.A.   1-267

To the young ladies of my house:

Alison, Sara, and Lucretia

Contents

Foreword   ix

I INTRODUCTION: The Contours of a Pilgrimage   1

II Mark 14:62: The End Product of a Christian
     Pesher Tradition?   10
     Postscript   18

III The Son of Man in Ancient Judaism and Primitive
     Christianity: A Suggestion   23
     Postscript   36

IV Recent Trends in Research in the Christology of the
     New Testament   41

V The Son of Man in the Synoptic Tradition   57
     Postscript   83

VI The Creative Use of the Son of Man Traditions by
     Mark   84

VII The Use of (Para)didonai in Connection with the
     Passion of Jesus in the New Testament   94
     Postscript   103

VIII The Christology of Mark: A Study in Methodology   104

IX Reflections from a Way Station   122

     Bibliography   133

     Indexes   143

Foreword

This volume is an attempt to put together the work that I have done on the Christology of the New Testament through the years. The title is an allusion to the *Festschrift* which a group of my friends and colleagues published in honor of my fiftieth birthday, *Christology and a Modern Pilgrimage: A Discussion with Norman Perrin* (1971), and to the essay within that volume by Victor P. Furnish, "Notes on a Pilgrimage: Norman Perrin and New Testament Christology."

The bulk of the material has been published before, as follows:

"Mark 14:62: The End Product of a Christian Pesher Tradition?" *New Testament Studies* 12 (1965–66), pp. 150–155.

"The Son of Man in Ancient Judaism and Primitive Christianity: A Suggestion," *Biblical Research* 11 (1966), pp. 17–28.

"Recent Trends in Research in the Christology of the New Testament," *Transitions in Biblical Scholarship*, ed. J. Coert Rylaarsdam (Chicago: University of Chicago Press, 1968), pp. 217–233.

"The Son of Man in the Synoptic Tradition," *Biblical Research* 13 (1968), pp. 1–23.

"The Creative Use of the Son of Man Traditions by Mark," *Union Seminary Quarterly Review* 23 (1967–68), pp. 237–265.

"The Use of (*Para*)*didonai* in Connection with the Passion of Jesus in the New Testament" in *Der Ruf Jesu und die Antwort der Gemeinde: Festschrift für Joachim Jeremias*, ed. Edward Lohse, Christoph Burchard, and Berndt Schaller (Göttingen: Vandenhoeck & Ruprecht, 1970), pp. 204–212.

"The Christology of Mark: A Study in Methodology," *Journal of Religion* 51 (1971), pp. 173–187.

These essays have been copyedited for consistency in style but they have not been revised. They are all reprinted here with permission. Where I wished to take note of subsequently published work or to modify my position today, I have added a postscript.

It will be obvious from the essays and footnotes that I am deeply indebted to a number of graduate students at the University of Chicago who have worked specifically with me on aspects of the Christology of the New Testament since 1964. They are as follows: Dennis Duling, now at Boston University, who worked on the use of the Old Testament in New Testament Christology, specifically in connection with the Son of David; Vernon K. Robbins, now at the University of Illinois, who worked on the Christology of Mark; Richard A. Edwards, now at the Virginia Polytechnic Institute, who worked on the Son of Man in Q; John R. Donahue, now at Vanderbilt University, who worked on the trial narrative in the Gospel of Mark with its christological motifs.

Other former students to whom I am deeply indebted for their constant discussion with me of my work, but who did not themselves work on Christology, are Werner H. Kelber, now at Rice University, and Joseph A. Comber. Two of my current students contributed a great deal to the manuscript in its present form, Waldemar Schmeichel and Kim Dewey.

I am grateful to the John Simon Guggenheim Memorial Foundation for the fellowship which made possible the final stages of the work represented in this volume.

Finally, three notes for the reader's convenience. The New Testament is normally quoted in the Revised Standard Version, except that I have used "Son of Man" for the "Son of man" of that Version. Publication details of all works quoted in the text will be found in the Bibliography. References to Tödt and Hahn are here given in terms of the English translations of their books rather than, as in the articles as originally published, to the German originals.

The Divinity School   NORMAN PERRIN
University of Chicago
January 1974

The Contours of a Pilgrimage

It has been a feature of my academic pilgrimage that "one thing has led to another." I began with Life of Jesus research and that led me to the Son of Man and New Testament Christology. The Son of Man is most prominent in the Gospel of Mark and that fact led me to Markan research and redaction criticism. In its turn redaction criticism led me to literary criticism and hermeneutics, the most recent phases of my interest and concern. The work on Christology, therefore, begins in the context of Life of Jesus research and ends in that of a literary critical investigation of the Gospel of Mark, and this fact explains some of its special features.

After the acceptance for publication of my first book, *The Kingdom of God in the Teaching of Jesus* (1963) I was invited by the SCM Press to consider the project of writing a full-scale treatment of the teaching of Jesus. No such book had appeared in England since the second edition of T. W. Manson's *Teaching of Jesus* in 1935, and in the meantime there had been such important developments as Jeremias's work on the parables, the post-Bultmannian "new quest" and "new hermeneutic," and the general acceptance of the method and insights of form criticism. All in all the time was ripe for a new approach to the subject. The project appealed to me but I asked for time to work first at the problem of the Son of Man. I was very conscious of the fact that in my doctoral dissertation, finished in 1959, I had done little more than accept and defend the views of my own teacher, T. W. Manson, on that subject. In revising the dissertation for its publication as the book *The Kingdom of God in the Teaching of Jesus* in the years 1959–61 I was kept from rewriting that section only by the realization that although I was unhappy with it I had nothing else to put in its place. So I let it go and turned at once to an intensive investigation of the problems connected with the Son of Man in the Synoptic Gospels, an investigation which occupied me almost completely during the years 1961–64.

I began by working very carefully through H. E. Tödt's *The Son of Man in the Synoptic Tradition* (1965; German original 1959), a book I had mentioned briefly and, as I now saw, very superficially in my *Kingdom of God* (pp. 109–111). As I worked through the book again—indeed, again and again—I became more and more impressed by Tödt's own work and less and less impressed by that which he accepted on the basis of the work of others. Tödt was one of a group of pupils of Günther Bornkamm in Heidelberg in the 1950s all of whom were developing aspects of Bornkamm's pioneering work on *Redaktionsgeschichte*: G. Barth, H. J. Held, Ferdinand Hahn, and Tödt himself. Barth and Held, like their teacher, worked on the Gospel of Matthew, and their work was published with his and translated into English as Bornkamm-Barth-Held, *Tradition and Interpretation in Matthew* (1963; German original, 1960). Hahn investigated the pre-Markan christological traditions with a view then to studying the Markan redactional use of those traditions. The study of the Markan redactional use will no doubt form an important part of a commentary on the Gospel of Mark he is writing for the Meyer series. In the meantime his study of the pre-Markan christological traditions appeared and has been translated into English as *The Titles of Jesus in Christology* (1969; German original, 1963). It is perhaps the most important book on New Testament Christology to appear in the last twenty-five years, and I am both deeply indebted to it and constantly in dialogue with it. Tödt took up the Son of Man material in the Synoptic Gospels and he accepted as true the general assumption that there was an "apocalyptic Son of

Man conception" in ancient Judaism and, further, he accepted as proven Bultmann's contention that Jesus had used this conception by announcing the coming of the apocalyptic Son of Man but that he had not identified himself with this figure. On this basis Tödt went on to investigate the development of the remaining uses of Son of Man in the early church and the redactional use of Son of Man in the sayings source Q and the Synoptic Gospels.

Tödt's work on the use of the Son of Man in Q and by the synoptic evangelists can only be described as epoch-making. In my introduction to redaction criticism as a method in New Testament scholarship, *What is Redaction Criticism?* (1969 edition) I wrote as follows:

> . . . what is new in his [Tödt's] work is the way in which he is able to illuminate the theology of Q, of various aspects of the traditions and of the evangelists as these theologies are revealed in their redaction and use of the Son of Man material. In this respect, Tödt's work both validates forever redaction criticism as a methodology and immediately outdates anything done on Son of Man in the synoptics before him (Annotated Bibliography, p. 85).

That is an opinion I reached in 1963 and which I still hold some ten years later.

What began to bother me about Tödt's book was not his own work but his acceptance of the assumption of the existence of a Son of Man conception in ancient Jewish apocalyptic and his further acceptance of Bultmann's solution to the problem of Jesus' use of Son of Man. It was uneasiness on these two points which led to my own first independent investigation of the problem of the Son of Man in Jewish apocalyptic and the New Testament. There was one point I had investigated earlier, namely, that of the ultimate derivation of the use of Son of Man in the New Testament. There were, and are, three possibilities in this connection: Daniel 7; the Similitudes of Enoch; and the Book of Ezekiel, where the prophet is addressed as Son of Man by God. I had determined that the usage in Ezekiel was not the ultimate origin of the usage in the New Testament, and I was convinced that the Similitudes of

Enoch and the New Testament were essentially independent of one another. Subsequent investigations only confirmed these opinions; my problem with Tödt's work was not that he derived the Son of Man in the synoptic tradition ultimately from Dan. 7:13 but that he envisaged an interim development of a Son of Man conception in Jewish apocalyptic in general. So far as Jesus' use of Son of Man was concerned I was beginning to develop the criteria for authenticity of sayings attributed to Jesus in the Gospels which I presented in the first chapter of *Rediscovering the Teaching of Jesus* (1967). Tested by these criteria *all* the Son of Man sayings in the Gospels were beginning to look dubious to me, including those accepted as authentic by Tödt who, as I have said, was simply accepting Bultmann's conclusions on this point. Bultmann's conclusions, and their acceptance by Tödt, and also by Hahn, were already being challenged in Germany by Philip Vielhauer, although on grounds different from those which I was beginning to develop.

The late T. W. Manson used to tell his students in Manchester, England, that there were two ways of arriving at viable projects for research: either to find a conspicuous hole needing to be filled in the current scholarly discussion or to find a conclusion of that discussion with which one strongly disagreed. Well, by 1962, I had found conclusions in the scholarly discussion of Son of Man in Jewish apocalyptic and the New Testament with which I strongly disagreed, but I had not yet found anything to put in its place. It was then that I came to read Barnabas Lindars's *New Testament Apologetic* (1961), a book I had ordered from a dealer's catalog because of its title without knowing anything of its contents. That book hit me with what can only be described as the force of a bomb. I had been wrestling with the problem of the origin and development of the use of Son of Man in Jewish apocalyptic and the New Testament and had become thoroughly dissatisfied with the consensus viewpoint represented by Tödt, but without being able to reach a viable alternative to that viewpoint. In Lindars's work I found the necessary key to the solution of one major aspect of the problem: the early Christians had reached the use of Son of

Man in connection with Jesus by reflection upon their experience of his resurrection in light of their reading of Old Testament texts, including Daniel 7, in a manner akin to the use of Old Testament texts in the Qumran *pesharim*.

With this insight as the essential clue everything else fell readily into place. The Christians had reached their earliest understanding of Jesus as Son of Man by means of a pesher-like interpretation of certain Old Testament texts, and the use of Son of Man in the Similitudes of Enoch and IV Ezra—the only places in ancient Jewish apocalyptic other than Daniel 7 where the figure appears— became explicable in terms of a constant reinterpretation of Daniel 7. Incidentally this latter view of apocalyptic literature constantly reinterpreting previous sacred texts was to receive strong support in Lars Hartman, *Prophecy Interpreted* (1966) although I must admit that Hartman is prepared to think of Jesus doing this in a way that I am not. I am much more skeptical than he is in the question of the authenticity of sayings ascribed to Jesus in the Gospels.

This particular stage of my pilgrimage is represented by the first two of the articles reprinted below. The first, on Mark 14:62, was read to a faculty group at Emory University in 1963, and the second, on the Son of Man in ancient Judaism and primitive Christianity altogether, was first read to a meeting of the Chicago Society of Biblical Research in 1965. Both show me developing the theses that, on the one hand, there is no Son of Man conception in ancient Jewish apocalyptic, but only the use and reuse of the text and imagery of Daniel 7, and, on the other hand, that the use of Son of Man in the New Testament begins in the interpretation of the resurrection of Jesus by Christians in terms of Old Testament texts, specifically Dan. 7:13; Ps. 110:1; Zech. 12:10 ff.

I had now solved the problem of the Son of Man in the teaching of Jesus—at any rate to my own satisfaction! As I saw the matter Jesus had not referred to the Son of Man at all; all the Son of Man sayings stemmed from the early church, the beginning was to be found in the interpretation of the texts of Dan. 7:13; Ps. 110:1; Zech. 12:10 ff. being used by the Christians in a manner akin to the use of the Old Testament in the *pesharim* from Qumran. I was now in a position to turn to the teaching of Jesus as a whole and this I did in the work ultimately published as *Rediscovering the Teaching of Jesus* in 1967. In that book I discussed the "apocalyptic Son of Man sayings" in some detail (pp. 164–199), developing the views I now held, but I left all other Son of Man sayings for future discussion. Such a distinction was possible because I was following the general scholarly practice of dividing the synoptic Son of Man sayings into three groups: (1) apocalyptic (or "future") sayings; (2) sayings with a present reference; and (3) suffering Son of Man sayings. I proposed to discuss the second and third groups "at some future date as part of a wider investigation of New Testament christological traditions." In 1964–65, when the manuscript of *Rediscovering* was written, I had visions of writing a Christology of the New Testament, a project I was later to abandon in favor of the more limited goals represented by the essays presented in this book.

My work on the apocalyptic Son of Man sayings had revolutionized my thinking about New Testament Christology altogether. I had now become skeptical about any use by Jesus of Son of Man and indeed of any use by him of a christological "title" such as Son of David, Son of God, or Son of Man. All such usages in the Gospels seemed to me now to stem from the early church and to have their roots in reflection by early Christians on their experience of Jesus as Risen Lord. Although I had reached such a position on the basis of my own work I was conscious of the fact that the change in my own thinking reflected a general change in scholarly thinking about the Christology of the New Testament. So when I was invited to contribute an essay to the celebration of the centennial of the University of Chicago Divinity School I took the opportunity to reflect in general terms upon this change in scholarly opinion, including my own. The result was "Recent Trends in Research in the Christology of the New Testament," the third of the essays (Chapter IV) reprinted below.

The years 1964–66 were almost totally absorbed for me in writing *Rediscovering the Teaching of Jesus* of which my work on

Son of Man was only a small part. But I was now teaching at the University of Chicago and beginning to experience what has become a major feature of my academic life: creative interaction in my own work with the work of some quite outstanding graduate students. In 1966 I was constantly in dialogue with three such students, Dennis Duling who was working on the Son of David Christology, Vernon Robbins who was working on the Christology of Mark, and Richard Edwards who was working on the theology of Q, and specifically upon the use of Son of Man by the Q community. When I had completed the manuscript of *Rediscovering* I therefore returned to the Son of Man in the synoptic tradition now not only working myself but also learning from the work of my students. The result was the fourth of the essays (Chapter V) presented below, "The Son of Man in the Synoptic Tradition," a paper read both to the Chicago Society of Biblical Research and to the Society of Biblical Literature in 1967 and published in 1968.

This essay represents my fully developed position with regard to the use of Son of Man in the synoptic gospel tradition prior to the particular contributions of the evangelists themselves, a position developed and presented in constant dialogue with other scholars and their viewpoints, particularly Tödt. In a sense it is the climax of the work I had begun by rereading Tödt in 1961, and I regard it as the definitive statement of my views. But these were views with regard to the Son of Man in the synoptic *tradition*; I had only begun to approach the obvious next step, the use of Son of Man by the synoptic *evangelists*, particularly the evangelist Mark. Moreover, I had not yet discussed in any detail the so-called suffering Son of Man sayings, i.e., the passion predictions and Mark 10:45, mostly because I realized that this could only be done in the context of a discussion of the evangelist Mark and after further study of the use of (*para*)*didonai* (a key word in the second and third predictions and in Mark 10:45) in connection with the passion of Jesus in the New Testament. These are the tasks to which I turned as soon as I had finished the paper on the Son of Man in the synoptic tradition.

The first fruits of this further work appeared immediately. The editors of the *Union Seminary Quarterly Review* had had access to mimeographed copies of my paper on the Son of Man in the synoptic tradition (the SBL met at Union Theological Seminary in 1967) and they invited me to develop further my work on the use of Son of Man by Mark in their journal. This I was glad to do and the result, "The Creative Use of the Son of Man Traditions by Mark," appeared in the summer of 1968. It was, and for that matter still is, too short and slight a paper but it did show something of the way my work was developing and it is the fifth essay (Chapter VI) reprinted below. In the meantime a further invitation had been extended to me, namely, to contribute an essay to a *Festschrift* which the students of Professor Jeremias were planning to present to him on the occasion of his seventieth birthday in 1970. For this occasion I turned to the use of (*para*)*didonai* in connection with the passion of Jesus in the New Testament. This was appropriate because Jeremias himself had been in debate with Tödt and Hahn on aspects of this matter, and it was also important to me to pin down the pre-Markan and non-Markan uses of (*para*)*didonai* in connection with the passion of Jesus in the New Testament. The result was a short essay, the sixth (Chapter VII) reprinted below, but one which I regard as of some importance since its conclusions became fundamental to me in my attack upon the problems of the use of Son of Man by Mark in general and upon those of the suffering Son of Man sayings in particular.

At this point the problems of Christology and the Son of Man in the New Testament become the problems of the interpretation of the Gospel of Mark, and by 1970 my interest was turning from Christology and the Son of Man to the interpretation of the Gospel of Mark. But in the summer of 1970 I was enjoying a holiday in London with my wife preparatory to conducting a seminar on the Christology of the New Testament at the annual meeting of the Studiorum Novi Testamenti Societas, to be held this year in Newcastle upon Tyne in England, when I heard that one of the promised participants could not make the journey to the meetings. Since there was no one else I could invite on such short notice I simply disappeared into Dr. Williams's Library, well known to me from my years in London from 1949–52, and hurriedly put together a presentation on the Christology of Mark, a presentation in which I tried to approach that Christology in light of the techniques I was developing for the interpretation of the Gospel of Mark as a whole. This was so well received by the seminar that I subsequently wrote it up in proper form for publication in the *Journal of Religion*, and it is the last of the papers (Chapter VIII) reprinted below. It is not my last work on New Testament Christology, nor on the Son of Man in the New Testament, but it is my most recently published work on these subjects, and an indication of possible subsequent developments must await the end of the reading of the essays themselves. Such an indication will be found in the "Reflections from a Way Station" with which I conclude this volume.

The essays that follow are printed in the chronological order in which they were written and published since the purpose of this book is to give an account of my pilgrimage in New Testament Christology. However, for those readers who prefer a logical rather than a chronological approach they might perhaps best be read in the following order: (1) Recent Trends in Research in the Christology of the New Testament (=present chapter IV); (2) The Son of Man in Ancient Judaism and Primitive Christianity: A Suggestion (=present chapter III); (3) Mark 14:62: The End Product of a Christian Pesher Tradition? (=present chapter II); (4) The Son of Man in the Synoptic Tradition (=present chapter V); (5) The Use of (*Para*)*didonai* in Connection with the Passion of Jesus in the New Testament (=present chapter VII); (6) The Creative Use of the Son of Man Traditions by Mark (=present chapter VI); (7) The Christology of Mark: A Study in Methodology (=present chapter VIII).

Mark 14:62
The End Product of a Christian
Pesher Tradition?

Attention has recently been directed to the possibility that there is an influence at work in the early Christian tradition in some ways parallel to that which we find in the Qumran texts so far as the use of the Old Testament is concerned. This has been argued particularly by Barnabas Lindars, *New Testament Apologetic* (1961), and personally I feel that his basic contention that there is a Christian pesher type use of the Old Testament is irresistible. A comparison of the Pentecost speech of Peter with 4QpPs37 has convinced me that the New Testament tradition does do exactly what the Qumran pesher tradition does: it understands and interprets events within its own experience and aspects of its own expectation in the light of Old Testament passages, and in so doing it exercises significant freedom with regard to the wording of the Old Testament passage concerned. The purpose of this particular study is to argue that Mark 14:62 is to be understood as the end product of a Christian pesher tradition.

The general procedure within the Christian tradition for which I would argue is as follows:

(1) There is a point of origin in Christian experience or expectation.

(2) This experience or expectation is then interpreted in terms of Old Testament passages as in the Qumran *pesharim*. This is the Christian pesher.

(3) The Christian pesher can then be *historicized*, i.e., a narrative can be formed from it or it can be read back into the teaching of Jesus.

(4) The pesher itself, or its historicization, can then become the basis for further theologizing.

I do not claim that this is a rigid pattern but that it is sufficiently evident in the New Testament tradition for us to take it seriously into account. The aspect I would want to emphasize in this study is (3), the historicization of the pesher, for I believe that here we have a significant insight into a tendency very much at work in the formation of the New Testament tradition and especially into the process that has produced Mark 14:62.

Before turning to Mark 14:62 itself, I must make one point about the Qumran pesher tradition: it features extensively plays on words. To give three examples:

(1) 1Qp Micah on Micah 1:6 has a play on nt^c "plant" and t^ch "stray" (Lindars, p. 15);

(2) 4QpPs37 1:8 f. on Ps. 37:11 has a play on ^cnwy "meek" and $'bywny$ "poor" (as have the New Testament Beatitudes), a play probably due to the fact that both words can mean "pious";

(3) 4QpPs37 2:4a has $'whby$ "those who love" for an orginal $'wyby$ "enemies" in Ps. 37:20, having by this word play completely changed the meaning of the original text in the pesher interpretation; the Qumran scribe has then read the interpretation back into the Old Testament text.

I would suggest that in the Christian pesher tradition there has been a similar playing on words, and I shall argue below that this accounts for variations found in the texts of Ps. 110:1; Dan. 7:13; Zech. 12:10 ff. quoted in the New Testament.

Now let us turn to Mark 14:62; "And you will see the Son of Man sitting at the right hand of Power and coming with the clouds of heaven."

It is universally recognized that this combines two Old Testament texts, Ps. 110:1 and Dan 7:13, from which it is sometimes further argued that Dan. 7:13 must here be interpreted as a going to God in an ascension and not as a parousia reference.[1]

My argument is that this verse represents the bringing together of two originally separate strands in the Christian pesher tradition: (1) having its point of origin in the resurrection and using Ps. 110:1 and Dan. 7:13; and (2) having its point of origin in the crucifixion and using Zech. 12:10 ff., and then being expanded by the addition of the parousia expectation and a further use of Dan. 7:13. (1) is reflected in the New Testament in Acts 2:34 and historicized in Acts 7:55–6 and 1:9. (2) is reflected in Rev. 1:7; John 19:37, historicized in Mark 13:26, and used as a basis for theologizing in John 1:51.

Dan. 7:13 has an interesting history in the Jewish midrashic tradition for there it is interpreted messianically in two different ways: (a) as the Messiah going to God from earth, e.g., in Midrash on Ps. 2:9 and 21:5; (b) as the Messiah coming to earth from God, e.g., in Midrash Gen. R 13:11; Num. R 13:14. In the Christian tradition both of these interpretations are also to be found. The pesher using Ps. 110:1 and Dan. 7:13 has the first Jewish interpretation of Dan. 7:13, the pesher using Zech. 12:10 ff. and Dan 7:13 has the second. For the sake of convenience in this article I will call these Pesher 1 and Pesher 2 respectively.

Pesher 1: a pesher interpretation of the resurrection using Ps. 110:1 and Dan. 7:13 in its first Jewish interpretation.

Let us begin by looking at Ps. 110:1 in the New Testament tradition. To use my terms, the point of origin is the resurrection experience of the Christians. This is then interpreted in the pesher manner in terms of Ps. 110:1, as has happened in Acts 2:34:

> For David did not ascend into the heavens, but he himself says,
> "The Lord said to my Lord, Sit at my right hand,
> till I make thy enemies a stool for thy feet."

1. J. A. T. Robinson, *Jesus and His Coming* (1957). The view is widely held in British New Testament scholarship. Robinson claims the support of C. H. Dodd, T. W. Manson, Vincent Taylor, T. F. Glasson and G. S. Duncan at various points in his arguments.

The resurrection is interpreted as Jesus being raised to the right hand of God in fulfillment of Ps. 110:1, and this pesher then becomes part of the common stock of Christian tradition. From this point there is an immediate historicization of this Christian pesher in the pericope Mark 12:35–7, as Lindars convincingly demonstrates (p. 47), and there is also further theologizing on the basis of this pesher, e.g., at Rom. 8:34; Eph. 1:20; and Col. 3:1. More important to my immediate purpose is the fact that Ps. 110:1 is linked with Dan. 7:13 in the Christian pesher tradition. This happens at Acts 7:55–56: Stephen's vision. I quote only verse 56: "Behold, I see the heavens opened, and the Son of Man standing at the right hand of God." This is obviously dependent upon Dan 7:13 and Ps. 110:1, dependent that is upon a Christian pesher in which the resurrection has been interpreted in terms of both Dan. 7:13 in its first Jewish interpretation and Ps. 110:1. I suggest that Acts 7:55–56 is in fact the historicization of such a pesher.

Acts 1:9: "And when he had said this, as they were looking on, he was lifted up, and a cloud took him out of their sight." This is the Lukan schematization of the ascension as an event separate from the resurrection (elsewhere in the New Testament they belong together as different aspects of the same event, e.g., 1 Pet. 3:21–22). It is dependent upon a pesher on the resurrection in terms of Ps. 110.1 (e.g., Eph. 1:20; Col. 3:1) and Dan. 7:13 (*nephelē*) in its first Jewish interpretation. I would argue that it is a further historicization of this pesher.

Pesher 2: a pesher interpretation of the crucifixion and parousia expectation using Zech. 12:10 ff. and Dan. 7:13 in its second Jewish interpretation.

Rev. 1:7: "Behold he is coming with the clouds, and every eye will see him (*opsetai*), every one who pierced him; and all the tribes of the earth will wail (*kopsontai*) on account of him." This introduces us to a new factor, for here we have Dan. 7:13 in its second Jewish interpretation, "Behold he is coming with the clouds" linked with Zech. 12:10 ff., "every eye will see him (*opsetai*) . . . and all the tribes of the earth will wail (*kopsontai*) on account of him." Zech. 12:10 ff. is also to be found in Matt. 24:30, "All the tribes of the earth will mourn (*kopsontai*)," and John 19:37, "They shall look (*opsontai*) on him whom they have pierced." The New Testament is concerned only with the Greek text of Zech. 12:10b, 12a, 14a, and seems to presuppose a version such as

> They will look (*epiblepsontai*)[2] upon him whom they have pierced
> and they will wail (*kopsontai*) on account of him
> all the tribes of the earth.

Such a selection from the original passage for use in a pesher would be quite in keeping with the pesher methodology as we know it at Qumran.

I pointed out earlier that a feature of the pesher methodology is the use of plays on words, and I would suggest that the *epiblepsontai-kopsontai* Zech. 12:10 ff. has given rise to a word play in the Christian pesher: *epiblepsontai-kopsontai-opsontai*, a word play almost inevitable in a pesher since it plays on both the meaning of *epiblepsontai* and the form of *kopsontai*. This word play in the pesher then accounts for *opsontai* in the place of *epiblepsontai* in the use of Zech. 12:10b in John 19:37.[3]

Now let me reconstruct what I believe to have happened with regard to the use of Zech. 12:10 ff. in the Christian pesher tradition. The point of origin would be what Lindars appropriately calls "passion apologetic." As part of the apologetic for a crucified Messiah it would be argued that the crucifixion fulfills Zech. 12:10, and the crucifixion would be interpreted in the light of Zech. 12:10 in the Christian pesher tradition, thus producing the

2. Barnabas Lindars, New Testament Apologetic (1961), p. 124, suggests *opsontai*, but this suggestion overlooks the possibility that this reading is the end product of a word play in the Christian pesher, as will be argued below.

3. Such a word play could also lead to a substitution of *opsontai* for *kopsontai* in Zech. 12:10b (see the third example of Qumran word plays above for instance of this kind of substitution in a Qumran pesher). This substitution has actually been made by the original hand of Codex Sinaiticus, which reads *kai epiblepsontai . . . kai opsontai* in Zech. 12:10b. I would suggest that this reading is due to, and is evidence for, the word play *kopsontai-opsontai* in Christian pesher tradition. It should be noted that Sinaiticus reads this *opsontai* for the usual *opsetai* in Rev. 1:7.

apologetic use of Zech. 12:10b we find in John 19:37—in a form
dependent on the word play in the Christian pesher: *opsontai*
for *epiblepsontai*.

The next step would be the addition to this pesher of Dan. 7:13.
This takes the apologetic a step further—the one they have seen
crucified they will see coming as the Son of Man—and this stage of
the pesher tradition is reflected in Rev. 1:7: "Behold (*idou*), he is
coming with the clouds, and every eye will see (*opsetai*) him,
every one who pierced him; and all tribes of the earth will wail
(*kopsontai*) on account of him."

If we consider this state of the pesher we notice that a new verb
connected with *opsomai* has been added: *idou*; added, that is, to a
pesher which already features a word play *epiblepsontai-kopsontai-
opsontai*. I suggest that this would lead naturally and inevitably to
the extension of the word play to this verb, and to the substitution
therefore of *opsontai* for *idou* in this Christian pesher tradition.
This would give us: "They will see (*opsontai*) the Son of Man
coming" which is exactly what we read in Mark 13:26 (Matt.
24:30; Luke 21:27): "And then they will see (*opsontai*) the Son
of Man coming *kai epiblepsontai . . . kai opsontai*.

My argument is that the presence of this *opsontai* is due to the
pesher process that I have outlined; it has developed out of the
linking of Zech. 12:10 ff. with Dan. 7:13 in the Christian pesher
tradition. Evidence in support of this can be found in the Matthean
parallel (24:30) which actually adds a quotation from Zech.
12:10 ff.: "And then all the tribes of the earth will mourn (*kopsontai*), and they will see the Son of Man coming . . . ," thereby
making explicit what is implicit in the *opsontai*. It should be noted
that the form of this quotation is due to the pesher tradition from
which it comes (cf. Rev. 1:7c); it is not taken directly from the
LXX.

Mark 13:26 therefore represents the "historicizing" step in this
branch of the Christian pesher tradition; it historicizes the pesher
by reading it into the tradition of the teaching of Jesus.

John 1:51: "You will see (*opsesthe*) heaven opened and the
angels of God ascending and descending upon the Son of Man"

would seem to me also to be an historicizing of this pesher, this time in a characteristically Johannine manner. It is the parousia pesher translated into the Johannine idiom with the aid of a further LXX passage, Gen. 28:12.

Now let us turn to Mark 14:62: "And you will see (*opsesthe*) the Son of Man sitting at the right hand of Power and coming with the clouds of heaven."

In the article thus far I have argued for the existence of a Christian pesher tradition (following Lindars) and I have concerned myself with two separate strands in this tradition: one using Ps. 110:1 and Dan. 7:13 in its first Jewish interpretation (Acts 7:55–56; 1:9) and the other using Dan. 7:13 in its second Jewish interpretation and Zech. 12:10 ff. (Rev. 1:7: Mark 13:26 parr.), attempting to explain the way in which these two strands came into being and developed. The question now arises—at any rate for me!—as to the place of Mark 14:62 in this tradition. If we are to accept the view that it represents Dan. 7:13 in its first Jewish interpretation linked with Ps. 110:1 (J. A. T. Robinson, *et al*), then it belongs with Acts 7:55–56; 1:9. Lindars himself argues for a modification of this view. Originally Ps. 110:1 was conflated with Dan. 7:13 giving us: "And you will see the Son of Man sitting at the right hand of Power," which referred to Jesus' exaltation; then at a later (but still pre-Markan) stage Dan. 7:13 exercised an increasing influence; the remainder of Dan. 7:13 was added from a text like that now found in the Theodotian version, giving us Mark 14:62 as it now stands and making it a reference to the parousia (Lindars, p. 49).

The difficulty with this view is that the last part of Mark 14:62 is not from a text like the Theodotian text of Dan. 7:13; the word order is not that of either Theodotian or LXX.[4]

It is, in my view, much more plausible to suggest that Mark

---

4. Lindars seems not to have taken account of a point made by R. B. Y. Scott, "Behold, He Cometh with Clouds," *NTS* 5 (1955/6), pp. 127–132, that wherever Dan. 7:13 is quoted in the New Testament the word order is changed to bring the adverbial phrase "with [in] clouds of heaven" immediately after the verb "coming," a change not made in the Greek versions.

14:62 is not an independent development out of the pesher tradition represented by Acts 7:55–56; 1:9, but a conflation of the two pesher traditions I have been describing. Indeed such a suggestion is more than plausible for it accounts for every word and every form in the otherwise puzzling conflation of Old Testament allusions in the verse. What has happened in my view is that what I have called Pesher 1 and Pesher 2 came together in the tradition, the force bringing them together being the fact that both use Dan. 7:13, and the resultant combined pesher was then historicized by being read back onto the lips of Jesus in the tradition.

On this hypothesis the verse is to be understood as follows: "And you will see the Son of Man coming with the clouds of heaven" is from the pesher tradition in which Dan. 7:13 in its second Jewish interpretation, as the Messiah coming from God, is linked with Zech. 12:10 ff., i.e., what I have called in this study Pesher 2. Note that it is in fact a conflation of Mark 13:26: "They will see the Son of Man coming . . ." and Rev. 1:7 "with the clouds" to which has been added "of heaven," a phrase readily added to "the clouds" in this tradition, as, for example, at Matt. 24:30. It is, of course, part of the LXX, Dan. 7:13, and its absence in Rev. 1:7 and Mark 13:26 is an indication that these references are not being taken directly from the LXX.

"The Son of Man sitting at the right hand of Power" is from the pesher tradition in which Dan. 7:13 in its first Jewish interpretation, as the Messiah going to God, is linked with Ps. 110:1, i.e., what I have called in this study Pesher 1. Note the relationship to Acts 7:56: "the Son of Man standing at the right hand of God." The only two changes are "sitting" for "standing" and "Power" for "God." I would suggest that these are independent variations in the Christian pesher tradition for the "sit" and "my" of Ps. 110:1. As soon as this verse was used to interpret the resurrection in the Christian tradition the imperative "sit" would be replaced by a participle, "sitting" being the most likely one; the "standing" in Acts 7:56 is probably due to a developing influence of Dan. 7:13 on the wording as this verse is related to Ps. 110:1 in the tradition, since the Son of Man in Dan. 7:13 would certainly be envisaged as standing. The original "my" of Ps. 110:1 would certainly need to be made more explicit as the verse was used in the Christian tradition and the evidence indicates that this was done either by using "of God" or, if this offended the susceptibilities of the individual scribe, by means of a circumlocution such as "of Power." At Luke 22:69 both are used together, clear evidence that both are present in the tradition.

Every part of Mark 14:62 can therefore be accounted for on this hypothesis; it would remain only to modify the *opsontai* to *opsesthe* when the resultant pesher was inserted in its present place in Mark 14:62. Probably the original tradition of the trial had the High Priest's question and the simple answer "I am," which is certainly all that the continuity demands, to which the remainder of the present verse 62 was added as an expansion of the narrative and an historicization of the pesher.

POSTSCRIPT

This article is the first statement of a thesis which has become the cornerstone of my work on the Son of Man in the New Testament;[5] a thesis which I hold as strongly now as I did when I first propounded it ten years ago. If I were to revise the article today I would put less emphasis upon the "historicizing" element. But in 1963 I was just beginning to accept wholeheartedly the form-critical view of the gospel narratives and was therefore interested in exploring aspects of the process by means of which early Christians expressed their convictions and conclusions in the form of sayings of Jesus and told stories of their lives as communities in the form of stories about Jesus and his disciples, and so on. In 1973 I am thoroughly accustomed to the idea and would no longer feel it worthy of special emphasis.

It is always difficult to pinpoint the actual beginning of a movement in the world of scholarship and I do not know who was the first scholar to realize the significance of a pesher-type exegesis of the Old Testament for the development of Christology in earliest

5. I elaborated the thesis further and in more detail in *Rediscovering*, pp. 164–185.

Christianity. Probably the best thing to do would be to say that in the early 1960s it was an idea whose time had come. My own indebtedness was to Lindars's *New Testament Apologetic*, where however the emphasis was upon apologetic rather than Christology. In the last decade however it is an idea which has been vigorously pursued, especially perhaps by Matthew Black and his pupils. In 1970 Professor Black became president of the international society of New Testament scholars, Studiorum Novi Testamenti Societas, and he took the opportunity to address himself to the subject in general terms in a presidential address, "The Christological Use of the Old Testament in the New Testament."[6] This is a most important statement of the current stage of the discussion but it is more than that for, among other things, Black may well have solved the vexed question of the origin of the Christology associated with the Aramaic *mar* of *maranatha*. He offers strong arguments in support of a derivation from a Christian interpretation of 1 En. 1:9 which is quoted in Jude 14, "Behold the Lord cometh with ten thousands of his saints . . . ," in a form very close to an Aramaic version of 1 Enoch found in Case 4 at Qumran.[7]

So far as my specific suggestion with regard to the origin of the Christology associated with Son of Man is concerned this has recently found strong support from two American scholars, Hendrikus Boers and William O. Walker, both of whom not only accept but offer further refinements which distinctly improve it: H. Boers, "Psalm 16 and the Historical Origin of the Christian Faith," *ZNW* 60 (1969), pp. 106–110, and "Where Christology Is Real: A Survey of Recent Research on New Testament Christology," *Interpretation* 26 (1972), pp. 300–327; William O. Walker, "The Origin of the Son of Man Concept as Applied to Jesus," *JBL* 91 (1972), pp. 482–490.

In my own work I have spoken very loosely of "reflection upon the experience of the resurrection" or the like, but it is of course obvious that the kind of experience associated with the tradition of the appearances is comparatively late rather than early. After all in

6. Published in *NTS* 18 (1971/72), pp. 1–14.
7. Ibid., pp. 10–11.

the matter of Christian origins the date of writing of 1 Corinthians is already "comparatively late." Moreover the idea of the resurrection of an individual was so new in the context of Jewish apocalyptic that there must have been some considerable preparation for it in Christian experience and reflection. What Jewish apocalyptic knows is the translation of individuals to heaven or into the presence of God and the eschatological general resurrection, but not individual resurrection. Boers, who had heard my original presentation of the paper on Mark 14:62, recognized the looseness of my references to "experience of the resurrection" as a weakness in an hypothesis which otherwise looked very promising, and he set himself to remedy it. In the process he made what may well be the decisive breakthrough to a correct understanding of the historical origin of Christian belief in the resurrection of Jesus and hence of Christian faith altogether. His own summary of his findings is worth quoting at length.[8]

> In agreement with Barnabas Lindars, Perrin states that "the interpretation of the resurrection comes first, as, indeed, we would expect, since without the experience of the resurrection there would have been no Christian theology at all. . . ." But the historian—as well as the theologian and even the believer—must ask what lies behind "the experience of the resurrection," which I assume means the appearances. After the shattering experience of Jesus's death on the cross, there must have been something which prepared his followers for his appearances to them from heaven, unless one assumes that the resurrected Christ appeared to them literally as now described in the New Testament.
>
> I have argued on the basis of three distinguishable layers of interpretation of Psalms 16 and 18 in Acts 2: 24–29 that it was Scripture that made it possible for the disciples to believe that, even though he died, Jesus was nevertheless the Messiah because he had been exalted to the presence of God. The second interpretive layer only, which asserts that Jesus who died was not left in death but was resurrected to appear before God, is relevant here. This understanding resulted from a combination of Psalms 16 and 18 through the presence in both Psalms of the Hebrew

8. Boers, "Where Christology Is Real," *Interpretation* 26 (1972), pp. 310–312, omitting the footnotes.

word *hᵉbelim* which only in the singular is distinguishable as two different words, namely, *hebel* (a line or cord) and *hēbel* (pain, pang). The former occurs in Psalm 16:6, "The lines have fallen for me in pleasant places"; Psalm 18:4, "The cords of death encompassed me," and verse 5, "the cords of Sheol entangled me. . . ." The meaning "pain, pang" is evident in Acts 2:24, "untying the pangs of death," which is evidently a mistranslation of an original "untying the cords of death," an allusion of the "cords of death" of Psalm 18:4. The latter verse states explicitly of the Messiah that he is dead, "the cords of death encompass me" but Psalm 16:6 says the "lines [cords] fell in pleasant places," and then continues in verse 10 to state that God "does not give me up to Sheol, or [let his] godly one see the grave." Evidently the Messiah does die, but he is not left in Sheol. He is resurrected to appear in the presence of God (Ps. 16:11). This supplied the disciples (with a clue to a new understanding of the death and Messiahship of Jesus. . . .)

The understanding of the death of Jesus which resulted from the combination of Psalms 16 and 18 prepared his followers for the resurrection appearances. These then became the real basis for the resurrection faith which continued to be interpreted with passages such as Psalms 110:1 and 2:7. And by the exegetical traditions suggested by Perrin the exalted Christ came to be designated as the Son of Man.

With this refinement I believe that my hypothesis becomes much stronger and that what I would gladly designate the Boers-Perrin hypothesis satisfactorily explains both the development of the "Christian experience of the resurrection" and the origin of the application of Son of Man to Jesus.

Walker's refinement concerns a later stage of my hypothesis, the stage at which Ps. 110:1 and Dan. 7:13 are linked in the Christian exegetical traditions. If the Christians were interpreting Jesus' presence with God in the light of Ps. 110:1 how did they get from that verse to Dan. 7:13, so that his presence at God's right hand becomes his presence there as Son of Man? Walker observes that there is a strong link between Ps. 110:1 and Ps. 8:6 (the endings of both verses are almost verbally identical). This could have led the Christian exegetes to Psalm 8. But Ps. 8:4 speaks of a "son of man" and this could have led to Dan. 7:13. This kind of

thrōpou, written by Carsten Colpe and not yet published, the manuscript of which I have been privileged to read.[2] These works naturally represent a variety of differing viewpoints, yet they all agree on one point: there existed in ancient Judaism a defined concept of the apocalyptic Son of Man, the concept of a heavenly redeemer figure whose coming to earth as judge would be a feature of the drama of the End time.

In this respect Tödt is typical. He has a heading for the first chapter of his book, "The transcendent sovereignty of the Son of Man in Jewish apocalyptic literature," and in his subsequent discussion he assumes that there is a unified and consistent conception which reveals itself in various ways in Daniel 7, 1 Enoch 37–71 (the Similitudes), and 4 Ezra 13: the conception of a transcendent bringer of salvation, the Son of Man. He sees that there are differences between Daniel and 1 Enoch on the one hand and 4 Ezra on the other, such as to suggest that there is not in fact a unified and consistent conception in Jewish apocalyptic, but he argues that in any case a conception did develop in early Christianity in which consistency was achieved and differences disappeared. This enables him to conclude his chapter with a summary of the elements which he regards as common to the different seers. Their vision is of a heavenly being, a savior to whom are ascribed supernatural and even divine powers and functions. His sovereignty and power are not those of an earthly being, as could be the case with the Messiah, but come from the future, from the Second Aeon. The seers' conception is characterized by a strict dualism which radically distinguishes between the present and the coming Aeon, and which determines the transcendental character of the conception of the sovereignty of this redeemer figure.[3]

---

79 (1960), pp. 119–129; Schweizer, "The Son of Man Again," *NTS* 9 (1963), pp. 256–261; Howard Teeple, "The Origin of the Son of Man Christology," *JBL* 84 (1965), pp. 213–250.

2. Subsequently published in *TWNT* VIII (1969), pp. 403–481.

3. H. E. Tödt, *Son of Man,* pp. 22, 30–31. Cf. Reginald H. Fuller, *Foundations,* pp. 34–43; and, in more summary form, Ferdinand Hahn, *Titles,* p. 17; Vielhauer, *Festschrift für Günther Dehn,* p. 52; Eberhard Jüngel, *Paulus und Jesus,* pp. 246 ff.; A. J. B. Higgins, *Jesus and the Son of Man,* p. 15.

Despite the widespread acceptance of this assumption there seems to be a number of difficulties with it.

In the first place, neither of the two cycles of tradition using Son of Man subsequent to Daniel 7 in Jewish apocalyptic introduces Son of Man as an independent conception with a title which is in itself a sufficient designation; rather, each cycle begins afresh with clear and careful references to Daniel 7. Whether we regard 1 Enoch 70, 71 as the climax of the Similitudes or as the earliest use of Son of Man in the Enoch saga, this remains true, for 1 Enoch 71 has clear references to Daniel 7 (e.g., verses 2, 10) and 1 Enoch 46, where Son of Man is first introduced in the Similitudes as they now stand, is virtually a midrash on Dan. 7:13. 4 Ezra 13:3 carefully identifies its "as it were the form of a man," which comes from the sea, as the one who flies "with the clouds of heaven," i.e., as the Son of Man from Dan. 7:13.

Further, the differences between the Son of Man in 1 Enoch and the Man from the sea in 4 Ezra are such that the reference to Dan. 7:13 is the only thing they have in common apart from the fact that preexistence, in the special apocalyptic sense, is ascribed to both figures, as it is in Judaism to many things. In view of the fact that 4 Ezra 13 does not have a titular use of Son of Man at all, we are not justified in regarding this passage as supplementing 1 Enoch in references to a Son of Man concept. Having identified its Man from the sea with the figure from Dan. 7:13, it then goes on to refer to him as "the same Man" (verse 12), "a Man from the sea" (verses 25, 51), "a Man" (verse 32), but never as "Son of Man." As for the distinction between the sovereignty and powers of the (earthly) Messiah and those of the (preexistent, heavenly) Son of Man, it should be noted that although 4 Ezra 13:26 has the Man from the sea being kept "many ages" by the Most High, the description of the redemptive activity of this figure in verses 9 ff. is couched in language drawn largely from Ps. Sol. 17, a description of the activity of the (earthly) Messiah. 4 Ezra 13 is, in fact, a kind of apocalyptic midrash on the passages concerning the Davidic Messiah from Ps. Sol. 17. In the course of this midrash the author uses imagery taken from Dan. 7:13, but the activity and function of the redeemer figure is derived from Ps. Sol. 17, not from any concept 4 Ezra can be said to have in common with 1 Enoch.

The weakness of the hypothesis of the existence in ancient Judaism of an "apocalyptic Son of Man" concept has not, of course, been overlooked, even by the scholars who hold to it. Tödt, as we have already noted, sees that the differences between 1 Enoch and 4 Ezra are such as to question the validity of the hypothesis but argues that in any case a conception did develop in early Christianity in which consistency was achieved and differences disappeared. This enables him to describe his concept in terms taken indiscriminately from Daniel, 1 Enoch, 4 Ezra, and the New Testament, without further inquiry into the differences and without investigation of special factors which might have been operating in one tradition and not in another. Colpe has a variation on this thesis. He freely admits that no "apocalyptic Son of Man concept" can be derived from Daniel, 1 Enoch, and 4 Ezra, but he argues for a fourth Jewish source, now represented by sayings in the earlier strata of the synoptic tradition but otherwise lost, and derives his concept from the four sources combined. Again, no further attention is paid to differences, and no inquiry is made into special factors at work in one tradition and not another.

It seems to me, however, that the time has come to question the validity of the hypothesis altogether. This I propose to do now, not by laboring the difficulties connected with it—these are obvious enough to anyone who has worked on the problem—but by proposing an alternative hypothesis which, in my view, better explains the data. This alternative hypothesis—my suggestion with regard to "Son of Man" in ancient Judaism and primitive Christianity—is that there is no "Son of Man concept" but rather a variety of uses of Son of Man imagery. Moreover, the use of this imagery is not restricted to Jewish apocalyptic and the New Testament but continues on into the midrashic traditions. Let me now outline the process which went on, as I envisage it.

THE BOOK OF DANIEL

Daniel 7 takes up an existing image from ancient Canaanite mythology, the nearest parallels to which, in texts now available to us, are from Ugarit and Tyre.[4] This image is to be found in Dan. 7:9, 10, 13, 14, which because of the metric structure is to be distinguished from the remainder of the chapter. It is the account of an assembly of gods at which authority is passed from one god, designated Ancient of Days, to another, younger god, designated Son of Man. This existing image the author of Daniel weaves into his vision, a procedure altogether characteristic of apocalyptic literature, and then goes on to offer his interpretation of the Son of Man figure (verse 27). It represents "the people of the saints of the Most High," almost certainly the Maccabean martyrs. The Son of Man's coming to dominion, glory, and greatness is their coming to their reward for the sufferings they have endured. In other words, the use of Son of Man in Daniel is a cryptic way of assuring the (Maccabean) readers of the book that their suffering will not go unrewarded. In exactly the same way the Christian apocalyptic seer uses a vision of white robed figures "before the throne and before the Lamb" (Revelation 7) to assure the persecuted Christians that their suffering will not go unrewarded. In all probability the author of Daniel was attracted to the mythological scene he uses because it is a cryptic reference to a giving of power and glory, and therefore will bear his message, and also because it has in it a mysterious figure which he can set in contrast to the beasts of his vision. That the figure is "one like the Son of Man" is probably a pure accident; any other cryptically designated figure

4. Endless possibilities from the history of religions and from Jewish speculative theology have been proposed as the origin of the Son of Man figure in Jewish apocalyptic. Two recent articles have pointed strongly to Ugarit and Tyre: L. Rost, "Zur Deutung des Menschensohnes in Daniel 7," in *Gott und die Götter: Festgabe für Erich Fascher* (Berlin: Evangelische Verlagsanstalt, 1958), pp. 41–43 (Ugarit) and J. Morgenstern, "The 'Son of Man' of Dan. 7:13–14—A New Interpretation," *JBL* 80 (1961), pp. 65–77 (Tyre). Carsten Colpe, himself a *Religionsgeschichtler* of real standing, has investigated thoroughly all the proposed possibilities and reached the conclusion that this "Canaanite hypothesis" comes nearest to meeting the needs of the case, so far as our present knowledge goes. *TWNT* VIII.

would have served his purpose equally well. His purpose was to bring to his readers a message of assurance, of power and glory to be theirs as a reward for their constancy, and nothing more should be read into his use of this Son of Man imagery than that. But Daniel becomes the fountainhead of a stream of apocalyptic and, like much else in the book, the Son of Man scene is taken up and used by subsequent seers.

1 ENOCH

The first use of the imagery from Daniel 7 in subsequent apocalyptic is in 1 Enoch 70–71. I accept Matthew Black's contention that this is earlier than the remainder of the Similitudes, that it is in fact the third of three descriptions of the "call" of Enoch (14:8 ff., 60, 70–71), each of which is built upon the model of Ezekiel 1 and describes Enoch's call to a different task.[5] These are not doublets but rather developments going on within an ever expanding Enoch saga.

The Enoch saga is a major development in Jewish apocalyptic, inspired by the cryptic references to Enoch in the Old Testament, especially Gen. 5:24: "Enoch walked with God; and he was not, for God took him." Indeed, the "call" of Enoch in 1 Enoch 70–71 is an elaboration of the second part of this verse, i.e., the reference to Enoch's translation to heaven, with a characteristic use of existing imagery, in this instance, Ezekiel 1 and Daniel 7. From Ezekiel 1 come the chariots of the spirit (70:2), the flaming cherubim (71:7), the fire which girdles the house (71:6; in Ezekiel fire surrounds the cherubim); and Enoch, like Ezekiel, falls to the ground when confronted by the vision (71:11; Ezek. 1:28). From Daniel 7 come the stream(s) of fire (71:2), the Head of Days (71:10) and, above all, the use of the Son of Man in connection with Enoch. It is easy enough to see what has happened: the seer has interpreted the translation of Enoch in terms of the call of Ezekiel and of the appearance before the Ancient of

5. Matthew Black, "Eschatology of the Similitudes of Enoch," *JTS* (n.s.), 4 (1953), pp. 1–10.

Days of the Son of Man. This was no doubt the easier because in Ezek. 2:1 Ezekiel is addressed as Son of Man; indeed, that use of Son of Man may well have been the connecting link for the seer, that which brought together for him the two scenes he uses in connection with the translation of his hero. Because the translation of Enoch is interpreted in terms of Dan. 7:13, Enoch becomes the Son of Man.

Daniel 7 and the figure of the Son of Man having been introduced into the Enoch saga in this way, they come to play a major role in that part of the saga we call the Similitudes. In Enoch 46 the scene from Daniel 7 is taken up again and attention focused anew on the Son of Man, who now for the seer is Enoch. Significantly, the first thing said about him is that he has "righteousness" (46:3), which is surely an allusion to Gen. 5:22, 24 where Enoch "walked with God" (MT), "was well pleasing to God" (LXX). At this point the characteristic concerns of apocalyptic come to the fore and Enoch–Son of Man reveals "the treasures that are hidden," namely, the way in which through him the wicked shall be destroyed, and the passage moves on to concentrate upon the coming destruction of the wicked. In connection with this revealing of the hidden we must remember that the basis for the work of the apocalyptic seer is always the idea that the things which will make up the drama of the End time already exist, so to speak, in prototype, in "the heavens," where they await the moment of their revealing. An apocalyptic seer is granted a vision of these things prior to their being revealed to all the world at the End; hence, he has a message concerning the End to bring to his audience. In this sense all the features of the End are preexistent, including the New Jerusalem of 4 Ezra and the Christian apocalypse, and these are the hidden treasures which are revealed to Enoch.

In 1 En. 48:2 the Son of Man–Ancient of Days imagery is taken up again, and the Son of Man is further distinguished as the one whose role had been determined (48:3). We are on the way to an assertion that he is preexistent in the heavens, awaiting his revelation at the End. The role of the Son of Man is elaborated in terms taken from the prophetic books of the Old Testament, especially Isaiah, and in the course of this elaboration of the role of the Son of Man, his preexistence, in this apocalyptic sense, is affirmed (48:60), and he is further identified with the Messiah (48:10).

The imagery from Daniel 7 is taken up for a third time in 62:5. Here the seer depicts the distress of the kings and the mighty when they see the Son of Man "sitting on the throne of his glory." Clearly he has in mind Dan. 7:14, and he is expressing the idea of the dominion, glory, and kingdom of the Son of Man from that verse in these terms. With his mind set on the Son of Man on his throne, the seer proceeds to elaborate the role of the Son of Man as judge of the oppressors and as the one with whom the elect and righteous will dwell forever. Both of these are, of course, common apocalyptic themes. Normally in apocalyptic, God himself is the judge, but in the Similitudes of Enoch, the Son of Man assumes this function. But again the reason is the scene from Daniel 7. In 47:3 God himself is the judge, but God designated as the Head (Ancient) of Days. Precisely because the Son of Man is given the throne of the Ancient of Days in Dan. 7:13, as our seer understands it, he can assume the role of apocalyptic judge; indeed, this becomes his major role. Having assumed the role of judge, he can also assume that of leader of the redeemed community, which elsewhere is also the role of God himself (Isa. 60:19, 20; Zeph. 3:15–17).

The seer returns to Daniel 7 for the last time in 69:26–29, which is the close of the third parable and a kind of closing summary of the role of Enoch as Son of Man. The name of that Son of Man is revealed to the righteous, i.e., the (future) function of Enoch as Son of Man is revealed, and he sits on the throne of his glory and exercises his function of judgment. It is interesting that here in this summary we should have reference only to the revealing of the name of the Son of Man to the righteous—the characteristic message of hope to the readers of apocalyptic—and to the function of the Son of Man as judge. This latter fact, together with the sheer extent of the references to this function in the previous Son of Man passages, indicates that the seer is concerned predominantly with the Son of Man as judge.

What has happened in 1 Enoch then is, in my view, that, in the course of the development of the Enoch saga, the translation of Enoch has been interpreted in terms of Ezekiel 1 and Daniel 7, and Daniel 7 has then been understood as referring to the giving of the role of eschatological judge to the one represented by the Son of Man figure (a quite different interpretation from that given to this scene by the author of Daniel), which in this saga is Enoch. Then the saga goes on to elaborate on the theme of the judgment to be carried out by the Son of Man, although constantly returning to the initial scene, and in the course of this elaboration other ideas characteristic of apocalyptic, e.g., preexistence in the special apocalyptic sense, are introduced.

4 EZRA

The vision of the Man from the sea in 4 Ezra 13 is, as I have already suggested, a kind of apocalyptic midrash on the Son of David passages in Ps. Sol. 17, a kind of translation of these references into a more fanciful style of apocalyptic. In the course of his midrash the seer makes use of the imagery of Daniel 7 to describe the Messiah's appearance ("as it were the form of a man") and the mode of his movement ("this Man flew with the clouds of heaven"). It should be noted that this is the first time in the use of Dan. 7:13 that the phrase "with the clouds of heaven" is understood as referring to the movement of the Son of Man figure. In 4 Ezra 13, however, the movement of the figure is not from heaven to earth.

The argument that we have here a transcendent, sovereign Son of Man conception must turn entirely upon two points, that the Messiah here is "kept many ages"[6] and that he functions as a redeemer, for these are the only things in common between this figure and the Enochic Son of Man.

The latter point cannot be held to be significant. The central concern of apocalyptic is with the coming redemption, and the fact

6. R. H. Charles, *Apocrypha and Pseudepigrapha of the Old Testament*, II, p. 616 n.26, finds this sufficient to identify the figure with the Son of Man of 1 Enoch (following G. H. Box).

that two figures function as redeemers only unites them into some such broad category as "apocalyptic redeemer figures," of which, incidentally, there is a large number. This is especially the case in this instance, since the main thrust of the redemptive activity is clearly derived from different sources in each case. The activity of the Son of Man in Enoch has been derived largely from the concept of his taking the throne of God, while that of "my Son" in 4 Ezra comes from the description of the redemptive work of the Son of David in Ps. Sol. 17. Everything turns, then, upon the fact that preexistence, in the special apocalyptic sense, is attributed to both figures. But preexistence is attributed to many things in apocalyptic. If this were not the case there could be no Jewish apocalyptic literature, for, as I pointed out earlier, what the seer sees is always the things which the Most High is "keeping many ages," until the time of their appearance at the End. Because of this, I remain completely unconvinced that this one point will bear the weight of the whole "transcendent sovereignty of the Son of Man in Jewish apocalyptic," especially in view of the facts that Son of Man is not used as a title in 4 Ezra and that there are no other points in common between the two figures.

THE MIDRASHIC TRADITIONS

The use of Dan. 7:13 in connection with eschatological expectation does not end with the apocalyptic literature but continues into the talmudic and midrashic tradition, where it is also used in connection with the Messiah. Here the major use is a development of that found in 4 Ezra 13 in that the "clouds" phrase is understood as descriptive of the figure's movement; but it goes a step further in that the figure now moves from heaven to earth. This is the first time that this happens in the use of imagery in the Jewish traditions. It can be urged that 1 Enoch implies that the Son of Man will be revealed as judge from heaven to earth, but it is nowhere definitely stated that he "comes," much less that he "comes with the clouds of heaven." However, this now happens in b Sanh 98a:

R. Alexander said: R. Joshua opposed two verses: it is written, "and behold, with the clouds of heaven one like a Son of Man came" [Dan. 7:13]; while it is written, "lowly, and riding upon an ass" [Zech. 9:9]. If they are meritorious [the Messiah will come] "with the clouds of heaven"; if not "lowly, and riding upon an ass."

A similar understanding and use of the text is found in the *midrashim*: Tanhuma B 70b; Aggadath Bereshith 14a (Billerbeck, *Kommentar*, I, p. 957); Num. R 13:14; and also in Gen. R 13:11 where, however, the reference is to the coming rain clouds, not to the Messiah.

Finally, the midrashic tradition also maintains the original meaning of the text in that Dan. 7:13 is used as descriptive of the Messiah's coming to God, not of his coming to earth: Midrash on Ps. 2:9 and 21:5. 2:9 is concerned with the glory of the Messiah, and it quotes Dan. 7:13a, interpreting it in terms of the glory and dominion which the Messiah will be given by God; 21:5 is concerned with the manner in which the Messiah will come into the presence of God, quoting and contrasting Dan. 7:13b and Jer. 30:21 and then reconciling the two.

The above is, I believe, a complete account of the eschatological use of Dan. 7:13 in the ancient Jewish traditions. It can be seen at once that each use is accounted for; the developments envisaged are reasonable and the hypothetical relationships are smooth. What we have is not the conception of the coming of a transcendent, sovereign figure, the heavenly redeemer, the Son of Man. There is no sufficient relationship between the use of Son of Man in 1 Enoch and 4 Ezra for us to suppose that they are both reflections of a common conception. What we have is the imagery of Dan. 7:13 being used freely and creatively by subsequent seers and scribes. These uses are independent of one another. The common dependence is upon Dan. 7:13, on the one hand, and upon the general world of apocalyptic concepts, on the other. Similarly, the scribes of the midrashic traditions in their turn use the imagery of Dan. 7:13 in connection with the Messiah. Although they abandon the general world of apocalyptic concepts, nonetheless, they find Dan. 7:13 every bit as useful in their presentation of the Messiah as did the seer of 4 Ezra 13 in his.

THE CHRISTIAN TRADITION

How was Dan. 7:13 used in the Christian traditions? To interpret the resurrection of Jesus! Just as the scribes of the Enoch saga interpreted the translation of Enoch in terms of Ezekiel 1 and Dan. 7:13, so also, but completely independently, the scribes of earliest Christianity interpreted the resurrection of Jesus in terms of two Old Testament texts: Ps. 110:1 and Dan. 7:13. Just as Enoch became Son of Man on the basis of an interpretation of his translation, so Jesus became Son of Man on the basis of an interpretation of his resurrection.

It is no part of my purpose here to trace the developments in the Christian traditions in any detail.[7] Let me simply say that there are, in my view, three Christian exegetical traditions using Dan. 7:13, all of which have left their traces in the New Testament. They were, of course, very much earlier than any book of the New Testament.

First, there is an exaltation tradition in which Jesus' resurrection is interpreted as his exaltation to God's right hand as Son of Man, a tradition using Ps. 110:1 and Dan. 7:13. The clearest trace of this is now to be found in Stephen's vision (Acts 7:55–56), and it obviously underlies the ascension concept altogether.

Then, secondly, there is a use of Dan. 7:13 in connection with early Christian passion apologetic. As part of passion apologetic in connection with the concept of a crucified Messiah, the crucifixion is interpreted in terms of Zech. 12:10 ff. (as in John 19:36) and then this passage is developed along the lines that just as "they" (the Jews) have seen him crucified, so "they" will have occasion to mourn, namely, at his coming as Son of Man. This is exactly what we find at Rev. 1:7:

7. See "The Son of Man in the Synoptic Tradition," below Chapter V, and *Rediscovering*, pp. 164–202.

Behold, he is coming with the clouds,
and every eye will see him,
every one who pierced him;
and all tribes of the earth will wail on account of him.

This is related to John 19:37, because there is a common variant from the LXX text of Zech. 12:10 (*opsomai* for *epiblepsomai*).

Thirdly, we have the full-blooded apocalyptic use of Dan. 7:13 in Mark 13:26 par. and 14:62 par. It can be shown that these latter two texts are related to the second exegetical tradition. (1) They use *opsomai*, the key variant from the *epiblepsomai* of Zech. 12:10, and that this is understood as a reference to Zech. 12:10 can be seen from Matthew who *adds* an explicit reference to that text in his parallel to Mark 13:26 (Matt. 24:30). (2) They allude to Dan. 7:13 in exactly the same word order as that found in Rev. 1:7, i.e., with the "clouds" phrase brought next to the verb. This is a word order not found in any version of Dan. 7:13 or in any allusion to it outside the New Testament. It is furthermore clear that Mark 14:62 is related to both of the Christian exegetical traditions, since it refers to Jesus, as Son of Man, "sitting at the right hand of Power" (from the tradition using Ps. 110:1 and Dan. 7:13) and "coming with the clouds of heaven" (from the tradition using Zech. 12:10 ff. and Dan. 7:13).

If the hypothesis I have advanced is correct, then it necessarily follows that there can be no apocalyptic Son of Man saying in the teaching of Jesus. All such sayings must be products of a church that had learned to think of and expect Jesus as Son of Man on the basis of the Christian exegetical traditions to which I have referred. It is my claim that a form-critical and tradition-historical analysis of the tradition bears this out.[8] The so-called "judgment-sayings" (Luke 12:8–9; Mark 8:38) and "comparison-sayings" (Luke 11:30 par.; Luke 17: 23–24 par.; Luke 17:26–27) do contain an element that goes back to Jesus himself, but that element does not include a reference to the Son of Man. The authentic element in the first case is a saying: "Every one who acknowl-

8. I argue this in detail in *Rediscovering*, pp. 185–202.

edges me before men, he will be acknowledged before the angels of God." This has a double Aramaism (*homologein en* and the passive as a circumlocution for the divine activity) and is a saying on the basis of which all other variants found in the tradition are readily explicable. In the second case the authentic element is a saying exhibiting an Aramaic idiom, the idiom of relative negation, in which the apparent exception is in fact an affirmation.[9] This saying should be rendered in English: "Truly, I tell you, no sign will be given to this generation. The sign of Jonah will be given to this generation!" This is the basic saying from which the others have developed in the tradition, interpreting the reference to the sign of Jonah in terms of Christian knowledge of the passion and expectation of Jesus' coming as Son of Man.[10] I give these only as examples of the way in which the analysis of the tradition, when it does contain an authentic element, shows an element having no reference to the Son of Man.

A further consequence of the correctness of my hypothesis would come in the field of the beginning of Christology. If my hypothesis is correct, then Christology begins with the interpretation of the resurrection as Jesus' exaltation to the right hand of God as Son of Man, i.e., with an interpretation of Christian experience in the light of Old Testament texts, rather than with the identification of Jesus as Son of Man in dominical sayings preserved in the tradition.

POSTSCRIPT

This essay represents the first statement of another major thrust of my overall contention with regard to Son of Man in ancient Judaism and the New Testament and, as in the case of the previous essay, I have seen no reason to change my opinion. As all

9. This idiom is pointed out by Colpe (TWNT VIII). He gives other instances from the New Testament: Matt. 15:24; Mark 2:17; John 1:11; 7:16; Matt. 25:29b; Luke 19:26b.

10. The work of my pupil R. A. Edwards, *The Sign of Jonah in the Theology of the Evangelists and Q* (1972) has solved the problem of the Sign of Jonah pericopes and convinced me that I was too hasty in my statement here.

scholars must be, I am grateful for the way in which Frederick Borsch has collected materials for us in *The Son of Man in Myth and History* (1967) and *The Christian and the Gnostic Son of Man* (1970) but I have problems with the methodology by means of which he approaches the materials and remain unconvinced by his thesis.

In my own more recent work I have been concerned with the nature and function of symbols and with the relationship between symbol and myth, being strongly influenced by Paul Ricoeur, *The Symbolism of Evil* (1969) and Philip Wheelwright, *Metaphor and Reality* (1962). In this connection I quote two passages from a paper, "Wisdom and Apocalyptic in the Message of Jesus," which I presented to a seminar of the Society of Biblical Literature in September, 1972.

We may begin with Philip Wheelwright's definition of symbol: "A symbol, in general, is a relatively stable and repeatable element of perceptual experience, standing for some larger meaning or set of meanings which cannot be given, or not fully given, in perceptual experience itself." A symbol is like a metaphor in that an image is employed to represent something else, but a metaphor does not function symbolically until it acquires a stable and repeatable meaning or association. A symbol can have a one to one relationship with that which it represents, such as the mathematical symbol *pi*, in which case it is a "steno-symbol," or it can have a set of meanings that can neither be exhausted nor adequately expressed by any one referent, in which case it is a "tensive symbol." Wheelwright distinguishes five levels of tensive symbols. The first two are symbols functioning only in one context or only in the work of one man (Wheelwright is, of course, mainly concerned with literary symbols). But the third is the "symbol of ancestral vitality," a symbol which has vitality through a long history of use, a category to which I ascribe "Kingdom of God." The fourth is the "symbol of cultural range," a symbol which has significant life for members of a given community, for example, the symbolism of the KJV of the Bible for the Christian (and post-Christian), English-speaking West. The last is the "archetypal symbol," a symbol which carries the same or similar meanings for most of humanity, such as sky father and earth mother, blood, fire, light, and so on.

In the case of the last three of these categories we approach what Ricoeur calls "primary symbols." For Ricoeur a symbol is a sign, something which points beyond itself to something else. Not all signs are symbols, however, for sometimes the sign is transparent of meaning and is exhausted by its "first or literal intentionality." It is clear that what Ricoeur has in mind here is very much what Wheelwright calls a "steno-symbol." In the symbol, however, the meaning is opaque and we have to erect a second intentionality upon the first, an intentionality which proceeds by analogy to ever deeper meanings. So "defilement" has a first, literal intentionality; it points beyond itself to "stain" or "unclean." But then we can, by analogy, go further to a "certain situation of man in the sacred which is precisely that of being defiled, impure." A symbol is then a primary intentionality which gives second and subsequent meanings analogically.

The function of "tensive" or "primary" symbols is to evoke meaning. "The symbol," says Ricoeur over and over again, "gives rise to thought." The opaque and evocative nature of the symbol is such that it "opens up" a field of experience to the human mind. In this respect symbol and myth are closely related in that they bring to expression, and tease the human mind into exploring, a world of meaning above and beyond that of perceptual experience, a world of meaning however which is existentially real at the deepest possible level. In what I have come to regard as a remarkable insight Ricoeur suggests that myths are to be regarded "as a species of symbols, as symbols developed in the form of narrations and articulated in a time and space that cannot be co-ordinated with the time and space of history and geography according to the critical method." We may say that myth narrates and in narrating uses symbols, or, alternatively, that myth narrates and in narrating comes to function as symbol in its power to evoke meaning at the deepest possible level of existential reality.[11]

To verbalize a symbol is to evoke new possibilities of meaning for the hearers, and the very fact that symbols are capable of different meanings by their nature means that those possibilities are not limited to one thing or another, nor are they readily exhausted. Moreover a symbol of the level of the ancestral symbol "Kingdom of God" necessarily resists objectification. Paul

11. See my essay in *Proceedings of the One Hundred Eighth Annual Meeting of the SBL* (ed. Lane C. McGaughy), vol. 2 (1972), pp. 554–555.

Ricoeur has argued that primary symbols, which would be pretty much an equivalent term for Wheelwright's "symbols of ancestral vitality" have to reach expression in the language of myth because the language of myth "has a way of *revealing* things that is not reducible to any translation from a language in ciphers to a clear language."

Let me explore for a moment the relationship between myth and symbol when we are dealing with symbols of the level of "Kingdom of God," or for that matter "Son of Man." The symbol is the central thing, plurisignificant, evocative of different meanings in different historical and cultural contexts. But when it is verbalized it is given a verbal context, and this verbal context is the myth. It is the verbal context of the myth which gives the symbol a particular meaning, although in the case of symbols of ancestral vitality the symbol always brings with it evocations of earlier and different meanings, and it still remains potentially capable of different meanings.

This can readily be seen in the case of the ancestral symbol Son of Man. In Daniel 7 it functions in the context of the myth of the reward of the martyrs, in Enoch in the myth of the redeemer being prepared for his work in heaven, in 4 Ezra in the myth of the redeemer carrying out his work in the world, and in Ezekiel in the myth of God addressing the prophet. In other places it can and does function in myths concerning primordial man, or concerning representative man, and so on. Now each of these is a different myth, and the particular evocation of Son of Man in each of them is different. But the symbol itself is both capable of different meanings, and it can also carry with it evocations of different uses when it is verbalized. It can carry with it evocations of so many different uses as are in cultural continuity. It is precisely because the New Testament is in cultural continuity with so many different myths using the symbol of Son of Man that the New Testament use of Son of Man can be so rich and varied.[12]

If I were to represent my contention today I would probably want to develop the thesis that Son of Man is a "symbol of ancestral vitality" in Jewish apocalyptic and the New Testament and that it is given its different functions by being associated with different myths. But this would not change the basic thrust of my

12. Ibid., pp. 553–554.

contention; it would rather make it more compelling by illuminating some dimensions of the way in which Jewish and Christian scribes derived the Son of Man symbol from Daniel 7 and then went on to use it in the context of different myths.[13]

13. Very recently one of my graduate assistants, W. Schmeichel, called my attention to the fact that the Jewish scholar Leo Baeck reached a position with regard to Son of Man in Jewish apocalyptic and the New Testament very similar to that which I later reached independently of him. His conclusions are worth quoting at length.

The images and words of the Book of Daniel still speak in all these [Jewish apocalyptic] books, either by being simply repeated or haggadically elaborated; nowhere is anything essential and new added to the conceptions of the Book of Daniel. It is nothing less than the apocalypse *par excellence*; and one of its important elements is the apparition of him "who is like unto a Son of Man and comes with the clouds of heaven and steps before God." Wherever in later works "that Son of Man," "this Son of Man," or "the Son of Man" is mentioned, it is the quotation from Daniel that is speaking.

In the Gospels, too, we see this clearly wherever they contain fragments out of apocalypses. When it is said here: "they shall see the Son of Man coming in the clouds of heaven with power and great glory," and "ye shall see the Son of Man sitting on the right hand of power, and coming in the clouds of heaven," one cannot fail to see that it is sentences from apocalypses, similar to that of John, that speak here, using no less than The Revelation of St. John, the quotation from Daniel.

Yet these two sentences, in which the old meaning is still evident, are overshadowed by the many other which show time and again that the word has received a new sense in the Gospels and has become a very specific term. It is no longer the ancient apocalyptic image that appears in it; it has become an independent theological concept; it no longer serves as a parable, as testimony of a vision, but to designate something specific. It is now the phrase which unequivocally denotes the Christ of the Church; used by him, too, to designate himself [according to tradition of the Gospels]. (Baeck, *Judaism and Christianity*, pp. 28–29.)

CHAPTER IV

Recent Trends in Research in the Christology of the New Testament

The occasion for which these essays are prepared (the centennial of the Divinity School at the University of Chicago) makes it appropriate for me to reflect on the current state of things in a particular aspect of our discipline: the study of the Christology of the earliest church as this is reflected in the New Testament. In this area some considerations have recently come to the fore which seem to me to be of great importance and to have far-reaching consequences for our work, and it is my wish to call your attention to them.

In the first place we have an ever-wider-spreading acceptance of the fact that sayings found in the Synoptic Gospels have a previous history in the tradition of the church. This is not, of course, new— Bultmann argued it and traced the history of many sayings in the tradition in his *Geschichte der synoptischen Tradition*, first published in 1921—but its widespread acceptance is new. Today, for example, Roman Catholic scholars talk about the three possible *Sitze* of a synoptic saying: the *Sitz im Evangelium* (setting in the purpose of the evangelist), the *Sitz im Leben Ecclesiae* (setting in the life and work of the church), and the *Sitz im Leben Jesu* (setting in the life of Jesus). In Protestant biblical scholarship such a viewpoint is now almost universally accepted. Many who would resist Bultmann find themselves inveigled into acceptance of

41

the approach by Jeremias's history of tradition work upon the parables,[1] and the recent upsurge of work on the theology of the synoptic evangelists which the approach has made possible is itself major testimony in its favor.[2]

The acceptance of the fact that synoptic sayings have a history in the tradition makes a great deal of difference to the study of Christology, especially in connection with the beginnings of Christology, because it raises serious questions with regard to sayings which have hitherto been held to tell us something about Jesus' understanding of himself and in this way to mark the beginning of Christology. Let us take as an example Mark 14:62.

> And Jesus said, "I am; and you will see the Son of man sitting at the right hand of Power, and coming with the clouds of heaven."

If this may be regarded as an authentic saying of Jesus then we can follow Oscar Cullmann: "He [Jesus] says in effect that his messiahship is not that of an earthly Messiah . . . but that he is the heavenly Son of Man and the heavenly High Priest,"[3] and go on from there to draw from this serious considerations with regard to the origin and early development of New Testament Christology. But if this saying has a previous history in the tradition then all this suddenly becomes inadmissible; the saying in its form in Mark is evidence for an aspect of Mark's Christology and earlier forms of the saying become evidence for stages of christological development in the church before Mark. Only the earliest form of the saying could tell us anything about Jesus' understanding of himself, and even that would only be the case after we had faced the question whether that earliest form is more likely to have come from Jesus or from the early church. In the case of Mark 14:62 the history of the saying in the tradition is in fact extraordinarily complex and the ultimate origins of its disparate parts turn out to be Christian reflection on the resurrection of Jesus on the one hand

---

1. Joachim Jeremias, *The Parables of Jesus* (1963).
2. On this see my essay "The Wredestrasse becomes the Hauptstrasse," *JR* 46 (1966), pp. 296–300.
3. Oscar Cullmann, *The Christology of the New Testament* (1959), p. 89.

and Christian passion apologetic on the other.[4] But it is not so much my purpose now to argue the details of the origin(s) and history in the tradition of Mark 14:62 as to point out that the acceptance of the fact that a saying, any saying, has or can have a history in the tradition changes everything with regard to the way we approach it, and the use we are able to make of it, in connection with the study of the beginnings of Christology.

A second consideration to call to your attention follows from this first one and indeed has already been stated in connection with it. If a saying has a history in the tradition then its various forms are evidence for the theological emphases at work in the tradition and its final form in a gospel is evidence for the theology of the evangelist concerned. In the study of New Testament Christology it was Bousset who first argued systematically that sayings attributed to Jesus in the synoptic tradition were to be treated as evidence for the theology of the early church. For example, in connection with Son of Man sayings—and Son of Man sayings would be generally accepted as the most important "christological" sayings in this context—he argues:

> In all our considerations we have no wish to deny the possibility that an individual Son of Man saying could have come from the lips of Jesus. But one cannot escape the impression that in the majority of these sayings we have before us the product of the theology of the early Church. That is the sure starting point for our work.[5]

The work that has been done since then has validated Bousset's argument a hundred times over. We might consider, for example, much the most important recent book on the Son of Man sayings, H. E. Tödt's *The Son of Man in the Synoptic Tradition* (1965). Over and over again Tödt is able to illuminate the theology of the

---

4. See my essay "Mark 14:62: The End Product of a Christian Pesher Tradition?" *NTS* 12 (1965–66), pp. 150–155, reprinted above as Chapter II.

5. Wilhelm Bousset, *Kyrios Christos* (1913). The translations of Bousset within this essay are by the present writer. An English translation of the book appeared in 1970.

evangelists, the theology of the sayings source and theological emphases at work in various aspects of the tradition by a systematic treatment of these sayings from this perspective. The way in which the tradition comes alive under this kind of treatment is quite remarkable and wholly convincing—at any rate to me! Let me give you just one instance, Matt. 12:32 = Luke 12:10:[6]

> And whoever says a word against the Son of Man will be forgiven; but whoever speaks [Luke: blasphemes] against the Holy Spirit will not be forgiven [Matthew adds: either in this age or in the age to come].

This saying represents *"la formule concise et succincte d'une importance maxime missionaire de l'église primitive"* (Anton Fridrichsen) and it tells us a great deal about the theology of the church from which it comes. First, this church has begun to think of Jesus as the one who is to come in glory and authority as the Son of Man and then to go on from this to meditate upon his earthly ministry as already having reflected something of this authority. Then, secondly, the saying reflects the church's eschatological consciousness of herself as the community of the End time, already possessing the Holy Spirit, the coming of which was to be a feature of that End time, according to Jewish expectation. Further, the saying shows the church reflecting upon the Jewish rejection of Jesus, who as Son of Man is also, of course, Messiah, and from both this rejection and her eschatological self-consciousness, deriving an impulse toward the Jewish mission. Finally, the saying echoes the beginning of a consciousness of the problem that was to haunt the church for decades, the problem of the comparative failure of the Jewish mission. All of this is clearly within this saying, and every aspect of it is abundantly attested elsewhere in the New Testament as a theological concern of the early church. The conclusion is irresistible: the saying is a product of, and evidence for, a stage in the developing theology of the early church.

6. In what follows I am developing in my own words insights ultimately derived from H. E. Tödt, *Son of Man*, pp. 114–125, especially 119, and from Anton Fridrichsen, "Le Péché contre le Saint-Esprit," *Revue d'Histoire et de Philosophie religieuses*, 3 (1923), pp. 367–372, especially 369, an essay not used by Tödt.

What is true of this particular saying is shown to Tödt to be true of the vast majority of the Son of Man sayings altogether, as Bousset had argued. I would myself go even further than Tödt and Bousset, for I am of the considered opinion that every single Son of Man saying is a product of the theologizing of the early church. Whether one accepts my radicalization of Tödt's position or stays with his comparative conservatism is, moreover, the choice that confronts one today. The kind of work that Tödt represents has been so successful that there is no turning back from its consequence: if not all, then at least the majority of the Son of Man sayings represent the theology of the early church. But Son of Man sayings are by all odds the "christological" sayings that have the strongest claim to go back to Jesus; if this is true of them how much more must it not be true of sayings using Son of God or Son of David? Today the burden of proof must be held to lie very heavily upon anyone who wants to claim that a saying expressing a definite Christology, or using an explicit christological designation, goes back to Jesus himself.

A third consideration playing a significant part in contemporary developments in the study of New Testament Christology is a concern for factors in the life of the early church to which developments in Christology may be related. Here again Bousset was the pioneer and we may refer once more to his work on Son of Man. He argued that the development of a Son of Man Christology was the way in which the disciples came to terms with the terrible problem posed for them by the crucifixion.

> They came to recognize that suffering and death was the only possible way in which Jesus of Nazareth could attain the exalted status of Son of Man. The cross was the means of bridging the gulf between the lowliness of Jesus of Nazareth and the heavenly glory of the Son of Man.[7]

The linking of christological developments with factors at work in the life and experience of early Christianity in this kind of way has come to be a major emphasis in recent work. A very good

7. Wilhelm Bousset, *Kyrios Christos*, p. 16.

example can be quoted from R. H. Fuller's recent and important book, *The Foundations of New Testament Christology*.[8] Fuller calls attention to a fundamental change in christological emphasis which has taken place between the stage of development represented by Acts 3:20–21:

> . . . the Christ appointed for you, Jesus whom heaven must receive until the time for establishing all that God spoke by the mouth of his holy prophets from of old;

and that represented by Acts 2:36:

> . . . God has made him both Lord and Christ, this Jesus whom you crucified.

In the first of these texts Jesus is the one who at his resurrection/ascension was predestined to appear as the Christ at the parousia. In the second text the resurrection/ascension is Jesus' exaltation and he has already been appointed both Lord and Christ and is already actively reigning. Clearly a far-reaching shift of perspective is involved in the difference between these texts, and Fuller faces squarely the question as to how, when, and why it came about. It is his answer to the last of these questions that concerns us: "Third, why? The answer must surely be, the delay of the parousia, and the increasing experience of the Spirit's working in the church."[9] This is characteristic of contemporary work on our subject; one of the most radical changes observable in the development of New Testament Christology is firmly and satisfactorily explained on the basis of factors at work in what may loosely be called the "experience" of New Testament Christianity.

Observations of this kind have a most significant consequence for the study of the Christology of the early Church, for they mark a shift in the focus of concern. Christology is now seen not so much as a product of reflection upon the past event of Jesus as upon the present "experience" of Christians. The church's develop-

---

8. R. H. Fuller, *Foundations*, p. 184. Fuller depends here on J. A. T. Robinson, "The Most Primitive Christology of All?" now in his volume of essays *Twelve New Testament Studies*, pp. 139–153.
9. Fuller, *Foundations*, p. 186.

ing convictions with regard to the resurrection, her consciousness of herself as the eschatological community, the necessity for an apologetic to Judaism, the delay of the parousia, the physical facts of movement from Palestine to the wider world and from a Jewish to a predominantly Gentile environment—these are now the kinds of things upon which we must focus our attention as we seek to delineate and to understand the origins and developments of the varying christological patterns reflected in the New Testament texts.

A fourth factor at work in the contemporary study of New Testament Christology is the impact of recent discoveries, especially those of the texts from Qumran and from Nag Hammadi. It has always been the case that scholars have concerned themselves with the "raw materials" of Christology, the materials available in Judaism and Hellenism which may have been used in the process of formulating Christology. The work of Bousset is here, again, epoch-making; he brought to his study of Christology "from the beginnings of Christianity to Irenaeus" the results of his own very considerable work, *Die Religion des Judentums*, and those of the immense labors of the history of religions school on Hellenism, and New Testament Christology was never to be the same again. Here in America his example was followed by F. J. Foakes Jackson and Kirsopp Lake, whose very important essay "Christology," published in 1920,[10] follows the pattern of focusing attention upon "the technical terms" (Messiah, Son of Man, etc.) in turn and begins the discussion of each one with a study of its use in Judaism/Hellenism. This has been the pattern followed right down to the present and it is here that Qumran and Nag Hammadi play their part, for they offer us a great deal of new information about the immediate environment of early Christianity in Judaism and Hellenism respectively, and this information will inevitably influence our christological studies. I have worked with the Qumran texts in a way that I have not with those from Nag Hammadi, so I will illustrate my points from these texts.

10. Foakes Jackson and Lake, eds., *The Beginnings of Christianity* I (1920), pp. 345–418.

The Qumran texts, in my view, raise the question whether we have not been too quick to think of titular conceptions in Judaism, i.e., of definite ideas and expectations bound together by a given titular expression which could be used by itself and would carry the ideas and expectations with it. Qumran introduced us to a new kind of literature, the pesher, and taught us how far and in what ways Jews could use Old Testament texts in the formulation of their expectations. This led me to question, for example, whether "Son of Man" exists as a titular conception in ancient Judaism and whether we should not rather think of a constant use and reuse of Dan. 7:13, 14 as seers and scribes of different groups formulated their expectations. If this should be the case then Jesus could never have referred to a coming Son of Man; the Son of Man expectation in early Christianity would begin with an interpretation of Jesus' resurrection in light of Ps. 110:1 and Dan. 7:13. I propose to investigate "Son of God" from this perspective also for, as is well known, this has never been found as a messianic title in Judaism. But it does turn up in Qumran in such a way as to lead R. H. Fuller to claim that "Son of God was just coming into use as a messianic title in pre-Christian Judaism."[11] But the context in Qumran is that of a pesher on 2 Samuel 7, i.e., a document in which a scribe is using that scriptural passage (with others) in the formulation of particular eschatological expectations, which leads me to question the use of "messianic title" here and to ask whether we must not seek a pesher-type use of 2 Samuel 7 (and related texts) in early Christianity as the basis for the formation of a Son of God Christology.

Thus far this chapter has been concerned with particular factors which I would claim are coming to the fore today in the study of the Christology of the New Testament and with something of their immediate significance for this discipline. Now let me offer you a change of perspective, and instead of thinking of factors at work let us think of trends which seem to be establishing themselves. This may only be to look at the same material from a different angle, but it will offer us a different view of it.

11. Fuller, *Foundations*, p. 32.

Perhaps the most spectacular of these trends which seems to be establishing itself in our context is what could be described as the movement from a concern for the messianic consciousness of Jesus to a consideration of a Christology which may be implicit in his message. Let me illustrate the change that has taken place here by adducing the testimony of two English scholars. The first is A. S. Peake, who is 1924 asks: ". . . is it not clear from the records themselves that Jesus believed himself to be the Messiah, the Son of David, the Son of Man, the Son of God?" He speaks of Jesus' consciousness of divine sonship attained at his baptism and argues that the motif of the messianic secret is due to the difference between Jesus' understanding of messiahship and the disciples':

> . . . It was far better that Jesus should lead them through intimate familiarity with Him, through watching His actions and listening to His words to form their own judgment of Him, rather than by premature disclosure to force the truth upon them before they were ready for it, and when they would inevitably have misunderstood it.[12]

That was A. S. Peake in 1924 and he was, of course, typical of his day.

Today a typical voice would be R. H. Fuller's:

> An examination of Jesus' words—his proclamation of the reign of God, and his call for decision, his enunciation of God's demand, and his teaching about the nearness of God—and of his conduct—his calling men to follow him and his healings, his eating with publicans and sinners—forces upon us the conclusion that underlying his word and work is an implicit Christology. In Jesus as he understood himself, there is an immediate confrontation with "God's presence and his very self," offering judgment and salvation.[13]

One can see immediately that a very great change has taken place, a change for which there are a number of pertinent reasons. One of these is that a view such as Peake's necessitates a great deal of psychologizing about Jesus. One has to speculate about his psy-

12. A. S. Peake, "The Messiah and the Son of Man," *Bulletin of the John Rylands Library*, 8 (1924), pp. 3–32.
13. Fuller, *Foundations*, p. 106.

chological and spiritual experiences at the baptism and temptation, about his motivation and intention in connection with the disciples and the High Priest, and so on. But such psychologizing and speculation are absolutely foreign to the sources themselves, for the Gospels never concern themselves with these things. Moreover, to fill in the gaps we have to supply material by analogy from the experience of other human beings, especially, of course, from what we can imagine on the basis of our knowledge of our own experience. The result is that we tend to end up either with a picture of a Jesus who looks curiously like ourselves—or as we would like to look—or with a picture of a man who seems to be suffering from delusions of grandeur. Which of these it is depends upon whether we accept or reject as authentic the more explicit claims to be found on the lips of the Jesus of the gospel tradition. The fact is that psychologizing about Jesus leads one into a morass, and this is a lesson that contemporary critical scholarship has learned well, so that today a view which involves this kind of thing would be generally rejected.

Another reason for the change is that critical scholarship now almost uniformly accepts the more explicitly christological sayings as coming from the early church. This is part of the general tendency to regard the synoptic sayings as reflecting the theology of the early church, to which I called your attention earlier. But the rejection of these christological sayings is not due to the acceptance of any vaguely defined general principle, of which it might be held that the opposite could equally be true; it is due to the fact that we can demonstrate that these sayings and their contexts reflect the characteristic concerns and theology of the early church, and that they are couched in terms characteristic of the liturgical and confessional formulas of that church.

There is today no going back from the basic change of emphasis and focus indicated by the difference between Peake and Fuller, and this is the more so for me because my own work on the teaching of Jesus has led me to a position like Fuller's, although perhaps slightly more radical. Let me therefore pursue for a while Fuller's concern, but in my own words and my own way. I have spent the last ten years of my life in *Leben-Jesu-Forschung,* for in the autumn of 1957 I began the work that eventually resulted in a book *The Kingdom of God in the Teaching of Jesus* (1963) and as soon as I had finished that, I broadened my concern to do the work which has resulted in *Rediscovering the Teaching of Jesus* (1967), the scope of which can be gathered from its subtitle, *The Reconstruction and Interpretation of the Teaching of Jesus.* How well or how badly I have worked in these years is not for me to say, but I can say that they have convinced me of the very real limits set to our knowledge of the teaching of Jesus. At the same time, however, our current knowledge of the historical Jesus and his teaching, for all its limitations in extent, is very firm knowledge indeed, and extremely unlikely to be shaken in any foreseeable future. We have sure knowledge of his teaching in parables, and of the general context in his ministry against the background of which these parables are to be understood. We know and can understand historically his proclamation of the Kingdom of God, although there remains the very real problem of how we are to interpret it, so to speak, existentially. We can reconstruct the prayer he taught his disciples, and appreciate the real force of the differences between that prayer and those of the Judaism of that day. I would claim that we can also understand the tremendous significance of his concern for, and table fellowship with, "the tax collectors and sinners," a group designation I would translate "tax collectors and other Jews who had made themselves as Gentiles." We can add to this list certain aspects of his challenge to discipleship, especially such as arise naturally out of the context of the kingdom proclamation. But when we have done that we have reached the end of our catalog. I am personally unconvinced at the moment that we know anything about his interpretation of the Jewish law or that we can say how he understood his own death.

You can see that I meant what I said about the limitations set to our knowledge of the historical Jesus. Yet I want to call your attention to what is surely to be regarded as a most significant thing: each of the major elements of teaching I cataloged above contains a surprising aspect of uniqueness, of boldness, of audacity. The parables include, for example, the parable of the Prodigal Son, which has to be understood as a parable designed by Jesus to defend his acceptance of penitent "tax collectors and sinners" in the name of the Kingdom of God. But if he did this, then he is defending an aspect of his own conduct by reference to the essential nature of the forgiveness of God. He is acting, and implicitly claiming to act, as I once heard Ernst Fuchs express it in a class at the "Kirchliche Hochschule" in Berlin, *"Als ob er an die Stelle Gottes stünde"* (as if he stood in the very place of God himself). The proclamation of the Kingdom of God certainly included the claim that aspects of the ministry of Jesus were the fulfillment of the age-old hope of the Jewish people: "From the days of John the Baptist until now, the Kingdom of God suffers violence and violent men plunder it" (as I would translate and interpret Matt. 12:32) is an authentic saying of Jesus and certainly implies that the kingdom is present in his ministry. The Lord's Prayer includes the remarkable mode of address to God, Abba (Father). Jeremias has shown that this is unique in ancient Judaism, that here Jesus is deliberately shattering all precedent, and teaching his disciples to do so.[14]

In all of this we can see one thing clearly: Jesus is *implying* a tremendous claim for himself and his ministry. This is the element to which Fuller quite correctly calls our attention. But there is a further element here to which attention must also be called: Jesus' words and deeds may imply something about the person of Jesus, but their actual authority, historically speaking, derived from the Kingdom of God. Jesus' authority was derived from the kingdom he proclaimed. Let me illustrate what I mean here by reference to the remarkable feature of the ministry of Jesus pointed out by Jeremias: the way in which Jesus addressed God as Abba and taught his disciples to do so. It can be argued that this usage reflects Jesus' consciousness of a unique relationship with God and

14. Jeremias, *Abba* (1966), pp. 15–67; idem, *The Central Message of the New Testament* (1965), pp. 9–30. The argument so far as the address to God is concerned assumes the comparative originality of the Lucan version of the prayer as against the Matthean, a point Jeremias makes convincingly.

his authority to bring his followers to share that relationship. But although this would be true up to a point it would be to put the emphasis in the wrong place and to miss the crux of the whole matter so far as the followers are concerned. In fairly extensive discussions of the Lord's Prayer in the context of the total message and ministry of Jesus[15] I believe I have been able to show that what the prayer reflects, and what makes the prayer possible, is the way in which the follower of Jesus had come to know God acting as king in his own experience, to enjoy the blessings of that activity as he responded appropriately to it, to find himself able to enter into a new relationship with God and his fellowmen because of what he believed God had done and was doing. In other words, the immediate reason for the follower's newfound ability to address God as Abba is not Jesus' consciousness of a special relationship with God but the follower's own experience of the kingdom.

What is true of the address to God is true of the totality of the message of Jesus: it implies a claim for his person and it reflects his authority. But if we concentrate our attention upon that implication and build greatly upon that authority then we are doing violence to the message itself. The authority of that message was derived from the reality of the kingdom it proclaimed, not from the person of the proclaimer. However true it may be to say that the person cannot be separated from his words, it is also true that the authority of the historical Jesus was the authority of the proclamation, not that of the proclaimer. True, as Bultmann is so fond of saying, in the early church the proclaimer becomes the proclaimed, and this shift soon had its natural consequences in a view of the ministry of Jesus in which the authority is that of the proclaimer, not of the proclamation. But this is the early church and we do well to be wary of this view in our consideration of the historical Jesus.

I feel it is necessary to sound this note of caution about the Christology implicit in the words and deeds of Jesus, but having done this I want to reiterate the fact that I share the shift of

15. See my book *The Kingdom of God in the Teachings of Jesus*, pp. 191–198; also my *Rediscovering the Teachings of Jesus*, *passim*.

and not from convictions concerning the Kingdom of God: (2) that the use in early Christianity is due to something Jesus said of himself and not due to an interpretation of Jesus in light of 2 Samuel 7 (and related passages); and (3) that a saying such as Matt. 11:25–27=Luke 10:21–22 is authentic, something that is quite impossible while the burden of proof lies upon the claim to authenticity, as it must be held to do today. So I believe that I am fully justified in claiming that the location of the beginnings of Christology in the early church rather than in the ministry of Jesus is a trend that is establishing itself in our work, and that there is good reason for this being the case.

If these two trends of which I have spoken are indeed establishing themselves then it is clear that future books on the Christology of the New Testament are going to look rather different from those popular in the immediate past. But then this, I would argue, should be the case.

CHAPTER V

The Son of Man
in the Synoptic Tradition

NOTE: The works with which I am consciously in debate in this essay are as follows: Reginald H. Fuller, *Foundations of New Testament Christology* (1967); A. J. B. Higgins, *Jesus and the Son of Man* (1964); Ferdinand Hahn, *The Titles of Jesus in Christology*, (1969); H. E. Tödt, *The Son of Man in the Synoptic Tradition* (1965); Philip Vielhauer, "Gottesreich und Menschensohn" in *Festschrift für Günther Dehn* (1957), pp. 51–79; Eduard Schweizer, "Der Menschensohn," *ZNW* 50 (1959), pp. 185–209; Schweizer, "Son of Man," *JBL* 79 (1960), pp. 119–129; and, Schweizer, "The Son of Man Again," *NTS* 9 (1963), pp. 256–261. The first and last of the three essays by Schweizer are also to be found in his collected essays, *Neotestamentica* (1963), pp. 56–84 and 85–92.

The two most important of these scholars for my purpose are Tödt and Vielhauer, for they give detailed expression of what I would regard as the only viable positions with regard to the Son of Man in the synoptic tradition: either all except a very small core of apocalyptic sayings must be ascribed to the church (Tödt) or all Son of Man sayings must be ascribed to the church (Vielhauer). What follows indicates that I now embrace the latter position. Other contributions to the discussion of the problem of the Son of Man in the synoptic tradition, e.g., those by Erich Sjöberg, are not taken into account here primarily for reasons of space.

The purpose of this paper is to present in summary form a thesis with regard to the origin and distribution of the term *Son of Man* in the synoptic tradition. Its title is a conscious allusion to H. E. Tödt's book, and it is my intent to present my thesis in deliberate contrast to his.

The starting point for this thesis is the work I have already published on the apocalyptic Son of Man sayings in the teaching of Jesus. In a book *Rediscovering the Teaching of Jesus* (1967) and in two associated articles[1] I have argued that the use of Son of Man in the New Testament begins in connection with an interpretation of the resurrection of Jesus by the use of Dan. 7:13 in a manner akin to the pesher methodology we know from Qumran. Let me restate my basic contention now without, however, restating the arguments that are to be found in my previous publications. It is my contention that the first christological step taken by the early church was that of interpreting the resurrection in the light of Ps. 110:1: "The Lord says to my lord: 'Sit at my right hand, till I make your enemies your footstool.'" This, in my view, is the origin of the *mar*-Christology, a strand of New Testament christological tradition isolated convincingly by Schultz and Kramer.[2] Interpreting the resurrection as Jesus' going to God's right hand in heaven, the earliest Christians came to believe that he was the one addressed by David as "my lord" in this text and so to call him "lord" in Aramaic, i.e., to call him *mar*. This they would do the more readily because, as Schulz has demonstrated, in Aramaic the title is used very rarely of God, but frequently of an authority with power to judge to whom prayerful representations are made.[3] Schulz himself tends to think that we have first an understanding of Jesus as Son of Man–Messiah and then the application of the title *mar* to him. But this seems to underestimate the significance of Ps. 110:1 in the process. The New Testament itself claims that it is because David calls him Lord in Ps. 110:1 that Jesus is Lord, and

---

1. Mark 14:62: The End Product of a Christian Pesher Tradition?" *NTS* 12 (1965/66), pp. 150–155, reprinted above as Chapter II; "The Son of Man in Ancient Judaism and Primitive Christianity: A Suggestion," *Biblical Research* 11 (1966), pp. 17–28, reprinted above as Chapter III.
2. S. Schulz, "Maranatha und Kyrios Jesus," *ZNW* 53 (1962), pp. 125–144; W. Kramer, *Christ, Lord, Son of God*, English translation by B. Hardy of *Christos Kyrios Gottessohn* (1963), Studies in Biblical Theology 50 (London SCM Press, 1966), par. 23, pp. 99–107.
3. Schulz, "Maranatha und Kyrios Jesus," pp. 134–139.

that, further, it is because that verse promises him victory that his residence in heaven is to be regarded as temporary: Acts 2:32; Mark 12:36; Heb. 10:12. Here we have, I would argue, reflections of the early theologizing by means of which both the concept of Jesus as *mar* and the expectation of his coming in judgment—hence *maranatha*—were in fact developed.

The use of Ps. 110:1 in the church to interpret the resurrection of Jesus is the beginning of an extraordinarily fruitful exegetical process in the course of which several fundamental Christian conceptions and expectations were developed. The exegesis of the verse itself produces the *mar*-Christology and the expectation expressed in *maranatha*. It is then further interpreted by the use, in addition, of Zech. 12:10 ff. and Dan. 7:13, and this produces the particular form of the *maranatha* expectation which we call the apocalyptic Son of Man expectation. The expectation of the coming of Jesus as apocalyptic Son of Man is a product of this exegetical process. According to my interpretation, Mark 14:62, with its allusions to Old Testament texts, actually reflects an earlier state of things than does Mark 13:26 where the allusions are tending to drop out and the expectation is tending to achieve simple categorical statement.[4]

The point at issue between myself and such scholars as Tödt and Fuller is whether the use of the apocalyptic Son of Man in the New Testament begins with a general proclamation of his coming, now reflected in such sayings as Luke 12:8–9 and its parallel, and then develops by the use of the Old Testament into the apocalyptic-type sayings in Mark 13:26 and 14:62, or whether it begins with the apocalyptic Old Testament-oriented sayings and then develops into a general proclamation. I would want to urge that consideration be given to my contention that the general proclamation of

4. In this connection one might note that the Christian Apocalypse seems to offer evidence of the importance of the Old Testament in this process. In Rev. 3:3 ("I will come like a thief") and 3:5 ("I will confess his name before my Father and before his angels") we have "I" forms of sayings which elsewhere in the New Testamnt are found using Son of Man, and the "I" in the Apocalypse is the Son of Man (Rev. 1:10: ". . . in the midst of the lampstands one like the Son of Man . . ."). But the seer identifies this figure by careful allusion to Dan. 7:13; he does not simply give expression to a general apocalyptic expectation.

the coming of the Son of Man is extremely difficult to locate in ancient Judaism.[5] I have argued that no such general proclamation is possible except in the one case of the Enoch saga where special conditions obtain.[6] Similarly, in early Christianity, the general proclamation becomes possible because the same special conditions prevail.[7] What we know existed, both in general Jewish apocalyptic and in early Christianity, is the motif of the translation of heroes and the use of the Old Testament to formulate beliefs and expectations. What we do not know existed is the general proclamation of the coming Son of Man.

APOCALYPTIC SON OF MAN SAYINGS

Having made that general point, now may I go on to face the challenge that necessarily comes next, namely, the challenge of showing how the general proclamation of a coming Son of Man develops from the apocalyptic Old Testament-oriented sayings of the type now represented by Mark 14:62 and 13:26. Here I shall concentrate on the small group of sayings which the current discussion would recognize as having claims to authenticity, including in my discussion Mark 13:26, but excluding Mark 14:62. It is among this group that Tödt and Fuller find the only Son of Man

5. Especially to be found in *Biblical Research* 11 (1966), pp. 17–28.

6. These special conditions are: the existence of a hero figure who has been translated to heaven and the use of Old Testament texts, including Dan. 7:13, to interpret that tradition. It should be noted that since I published my work, Geza Vermés's study, "The Use of *Bar Nash/Bar Nasha* in Jewish Aramaic," which is to appear as an Appendix to the third edition of Matthew Black, *An Aramaic Approach to the Gospels and Acts*, has been circulating. He argues very strongly, on the basis of the most thorough study of the Aramaic materials yet undertaken, that "Son of Man" was not in use in Aramaic as a title. This lends weight to my assertion that the phrase can only *become* a title when it is applied to a definite individual, Enoch in the Enoch saga, and Jesus in the Christian traditions.

7. The parallels between the Son of Man in 1 Enoch and the New Testament are to be explained, therefore, by the fact that two roughly contemporary groups in the same Jewish apocalyptic milieu have done the same kind of thing in the same kind of way. The Enoch saga interprets the translation of Enoch by means of Ezekiel and Daniel 7; the Christian traditions understood the fate of Jesus as a translation/assumption and interpreted it by means of Ps. 110:1; Zech. 12:10 ff.; and Dan. 7:13.

sayings which go back to Jesus. We are agreed that there are no authentic sayings apart from the possibilities in this group.

Luke 12:8-9: "And I tell you, every one who acknowledges me before men, the Son of Man also will acknowledge before the angels of God; but he who denies me before men will be denied before the angels of God." (=Matt. 10:32-33: "So every one who acknowledges me before men, I also will acknowledge before my Father who is in heaven; but whoever denies me before men, I also will deny before my Father who is in heaven." (Cf. Mark 8:38: "For whoever is ashamed of me and of my words in this adulterous and sinful generation, of him will the Son of Man also be ashamed, when he comes in the glory of his Father with the holy angels.")

Luke 17:24: "For as the lightning flashes and lights up the sky from one side to the other, so will the Son of Man be in his day." (=Matt. 24:27: "For as the lightning comes from the east and shines as far as the west, so will be the coming of the Son of Man.")

Luke 17:26: "As it was in the days of Noah, so will it be in the days of the Son of Man." (=Matt. 24:37: "As were the days of Noah, so will be the coming of the Son of Man.")

Luke 17:28-30: "Likewise as it was in the days of Lot—they ate, they drank, they bought, they sold, they planted, they built, but on the day when Lot went out from Sodom fire and brimstone rained from heaven and destroyed them all—so it will be on the day when the Son of Man is revealed."

Luke 11:30: "For as Jonah became a sign to the men of Nineveh, so will the Son of Man be to this generation."

Luke 12:40: "You must also be ready; for the Son of Man is coming at an hour you do not expect." (=Matt. 24:44: "Therefore you also must be ready; for the Son of Man is coming at an hour you do not expect.")

Matt. 10:23: "When they persecute you in one town, flee to the next; for truly, I say to you, you will not have gone through all the towns of Israel, before the Son of Man comes."

Matt. 19:28: "Jesus said to them, 'Truly, I say to you, in the new world, when the Son of Man shall sit on his glorious throne, you who have followed me will also sit on twelve thrones, judging the twelve tribes of Israel.' "

Mark 13:26: "And then they will see the Son of Man coming in clouds with great power and glory."

If we examine this group, then we find that they fall into several well-defined categories, categories which I shall call: "apocalyptic promises," "eschatological judgment pronouncements," "eschatological correlatives," and "exhortations to watchfulness." I shall now consider the sayings under these headings.

1. APOCALYPTIC PROMISES

The apocalyptic promise is a well-known feature of ancient Judaism and primitive Christianity. In it hope is held out to the faithful in promises which use God, Kingdom of God, Son of David, angels and archangels, and every other possible mode of expression for the intervention of God in human history. In this category I would put Mark 13:26, Matt. 10:23, and very possibly Matt. 19:28. The apocalyptic promise exists as a form prior to, and of course, completely independent of, early Christianity. As a form it certainly precedes the use of Son of Man in connection with it, since even if a coming Son of Man conception existed in Jewish apocalyptic, it is very rare in occurrence. Within the New Testament itself, apocalyptic promises are frequent in occurrence, but only occasionally do they use Son of Man. We could quote Mark 13:30, 9:1, 1 Thess. 4:16–17, 2 Thess. 2:8, and 1 John 2:28 as examples of apocalyptic promises which do not use Son of Man. In view of the close relationship between Jewish and Christian apocalyptic we must recognize that for the Christian church also the apocalyptic promise exists prior to and independent of the use of Son of Man in connection with it. I do not need to belabor this point because it would not be disputed, but I do want to stress that in the church the form precedes the use of Son of Man within it, for this will become a main point in my argument as it develops.

2. ESCHATOLOGICAL JUDGMENT PRONOUNCEMENTS

This is my term for Ernst Käsemann's *Sätze heiligen Rechtes*,[8] a term I have chosen because it seems to me to describe the

---

8. Ernst Käsemann, "Sätze heiligen Rechtes im Neuen Testament," NTS 1 (1954/55), pp. 248–260 (English translation, "Sentences of Holy Law in the New Testament," in *New Testament Questions of Today* [1969], pp. 66–81). On this extremely important form-critical investigation, see my *Rediscovering*, pp. 22–23.

function of this particular form in the New Testament. Whatever we call it, there can be no doubt that the form itself exists: it consists of a two-part sentence with the same verb in each part, in the first describing the activity of the man being judged and in the second the eschatological activity of God in judging. This form has left a marked impact upon the New Testament materials both in the Epistles and Gospels. The point to which I would like to call attention is that the use of Son of Man in this connection is neither original nor extensive. Of sixteen instances of this form isolated by Käsemann,[9] three use God directly in the second part of the judgment and two "your Father in heaven" (both of these in Matthew), five use the verb in the passive (a circumlocution for God very common in apocalyptic), two have an anathema phrase, two use the first personal pronoun with Jesus as the speaker, and only two, Luke 12:8 and Mark 8:38, use Son of Man. We have here, therefore, the same phenomenon as we have in the case of the apocalyptic promises: a definite form exists in the church and Son of Man is taken up into this form and used in connection with it, but the use of Son of Man remains a comparatively rare use within the form as whole. For Tödt everything turns on the one saying, Luke 12:8, as he himself freely admits,[10] but Vielhauer is surely correct when he claims[11] that this saying, like the other *Sätze heiligen Rechtes*, must be ascribed to early Christian prophecy. The minor role it plays within the form itself makes it extremely difficult to accept it as the fountainhead, not only of all eschatological judgment pronouncements, but also of the total use of Son of Man in the synoptic tradition.

9. 1 Cor. 3:17; 14:38; 16:22; Gal. 1:9; Rev. 22:18, 19; Luke 12: 8–9= Matt. 10:32–33; Mark 8:38; Matt. 5:19; 6:14–15; Mark 4:24. This gives a total of sixteen if we can count double sayings as two and ignore the question of parallels. This I have chosen to do because of the variety of usage within the four sayings represented by Luke 12:8–9=Matt. 10:32.

10. "Luke 12:8–9 indeed supplied the decisive impulse for our consideration of the problem of Jesus and the Son of Man." Tödt, *Son of Man*, p. 349.

11. Philip Vielhauer, "Jesus und der Menschensohn," *ZTK* 60 (1963), p. 147.

3. ESCHATOLOGICAL CORRELATIVES

This is a form isolated by one of my students, Richard A. Edwards, in his doctoral work on the Sign of Jonah pericope, in the course of which he investigated the theology of Q following hints and lines laid down by Tödt. He argues, I believe correctly, that a definite form is used to give content to the Son of Man expectation in Q. The form seems to be restricted to Q or to dependence upon Q and is a two-part saying introduced by *kathōs* or *hōsper* in the first part and by *houtōs*, or in one case *kata ta auta* (Luke 17:30), in the second part. The first part refers either to an event in the past or to a natural phenomenon in the present, and the second part refers forward to the coming of the Son of Man. A characteristic example is Luke 11:30: "For as (*kathōs*) Jonah became a sign to the men of Nineveh, so (*houtōs*) will the Son of Man be to this generation"; the others are Luke 17:24 par. (lightning), Luke 17:26 par. (Noah), and Luke 17:28, 30 (Lot).[12] This seems to be a form used in the church, and specifically in the Q tradition, to give content to the Son of Man expectation. The coming of the Son of Man is compared with past catastrophes, past acts of judgment, natural phenomena, in order to

---

12. R. A. Edwards, *The Sign of Jonah in the Theology of the Evangelists and Q* (1972). I will summarize some of the evidence for the existence of an "eschatological correlative" and for its particular association with the Q tradition.

There are six references to the future Son of Man in Q as normally defined: Luke 11:30 par.; 12:8 par.; 12:40 par.; 17:24 par.; 17:26 par.; 17:30 par. In four of these (11:30; 17:24; 17:26; 17:28) we have the correlative form with the verb in the apodosis in the future.

This correlative form (with a verb in the future) occurs only here in Q, never in Mark, never in Luke apart from Q, and only once in Matthew at 13:40 where it is followed by a Son of Man reference in verse 41.

John has the *kathōs* (*hōsper*) . . . *houtōs* form six times, although never with the verb in the apodosis in the future. Five of these have a christological reference: In 3:14 the form is used in connection with the Son of Man, in 5:21; 5:26; 12:50; 14:31 the reference is either to the Son, or Jesus speaks in the first person having referred to the Father in the protasis. John appears, therefore, to know and to develop the form in his own way.

Paul makes extensive use of the correlative, but only in three places does the apodosis have a verb in the future: Rom. 5:19; 1 Cor. 15:22, 49. In each case the comparison is between Christ and Adam.

give shape and content to the expectation. In this particular instance, therefore, we do not have a form existing prior to the use of Son of Man in connection with it, but rather a form created specifically to give content to a previously existing expectation. But since the expectation must necessarily exist prior to a form created to give content to it, the origin of the Son of Man expectation in the New Testament cannot lie in one of these sayings.

4. EXHORTATION TO WATCHFULNESS

The one other Son of Man saying in Q, Luke 12:40 par., is also part of a widely distributed Christian tradition. In this instance a metaphor has carried the tradition rather than a form. In 1 Thess. 5:3, 4 and 2 Pet. 3:10 we have references to "the Lord," "that day," "the day of the Lord," each of which comes "like a thief." In Rev. 3:3 we read "I will come like a thief" (see 1:13, 14); and in Rev. 16:15 we find "I am coming like a thief." In the synoptic tradition this metaphor has become a parable and Son of Man is introduced in a hortatory conclusion in Q (Luke 12:40= Matt. 24:44), but not in Mark (13:35–36). Whatever may be the ultimate origin of this parable,[13] the Son of Man saying is clearly an introduction of Son of Man into an existing tradition of exhortation.

I am myself very impressed by the fact that the only category of Son of Man sayings which exists as a category in its own right is one (the eschatological correlative) which is designed to give content to a previously existing expectation. Those who wish to see the original Son of Man in the New Testament in an authentic apocalyptic Son of Man saying must face the fact that there is no such formal category as "apocalyptic Son of Man sayings" in the New Testament. There are only apocalyptic promises, eschatological judgment pronouncements, and the like, which take up and use Son of Man in a secondary manner. So I would claim that the

---

13. Joachim Jeremias, *Parables of Jesus* (rev. ed., 1963), pp. 48–51, argues that the parable does go back to Jesus but not the saying using the Son of Man, that is "christological allegorizing." Vielhauer (Dehn *Festschrift*, p. 66, n. 79) argues that the parable is "*vom Haus aus Christologisch*."

origin of the use of Son of Man in the early church does not lie in any of these traditions but rather in the interpretation of the Old Testament. Of course, if the Son of Man expectation in a general form could be established as existing independent of any of these traditions or independent of the use of the Old Testament, then the same procedure would follow with regard to its spread in the Christian traditions. However, as I have already said, this is the point I dispute.

Another point I dispute is that we have in any of these sayings the authentic voice of Jesus. I find it very hard to accept the conclusion that we have the authentic voice of Jesus in sayings which clearly are part of an established tradition in the early church, reflecting the church's life and practice, or giving content to the church's expectation. Of course it is quite impossible that we should have the voice of Jesus in an exegetical tradition which is reflecting upon the resurrection.

I shall now recapitulate my thesis as to the origin and development of the apocalyptic Son of Man in the synoptic tradition. It begins with Christian reflection upon the resurrection in the light of Ps. 110:1, from which comes the christological concept of Jesus as *mar* and the expectation expressed in *maranatha*. Then Zech. 12:10–11 and Dan. 7:13 are introduced into this particular exegetical tradition to give the concept of Jesus at the right hand of God as Son of Man and the particular form of the expectation of his coming again which expected him to come as Son of Man. From this point forward the Q tradition gives further content to this expectation by the use of the eschatological correlative and the expectation is taken up in the church and used in connection with existing and more broadly based traditions: the apocalyptic promise, the eschatological judgment, and the exhortation to watchfulness.

SON OF MAN SAYINGS WITH A PRESENT REFERENCE

I turn next to the Son of Man sayings in the synoptic tradition which have a present reference. These are as follows.

Luke 7:34=Matt. 11:19: "The Son of Man has come eating and
drinking and you say, 'Behold a glutton and a drunkard, a
friend of tax collectors and sinners!' "

Luke 12:10=Matt. 12:32: "And every one who speaks a word
against the Son of Man will be forgiven; but he who blasphemes
[Matt.: speaks against] the Holy Spirit will not be forgiven."

Luke 9:58=Matt. 8:30: "Foxes have holes, and birds of the air
have nests; but the Son of Man has nowhere to lay his head."

Luke 6:25=Matt. 5:20: "Blessed are you when men hate you . . . on
account of the Son of Man!" (Matt.: "Blessed are you when
men revile you . . . on my account.")

Luke 19:10: "For the Son of Man came to seek and to save the lost."

Matt. 13:37: "He who sows the good seed is the Son of Man."

Mark 10:45: "The Son of Man also came not to be served but to
serve, and to give his life a ransom for many."

Mark 2:10: "But that you may know that the Son of Man has authority (*exousia*) on earth to forgive sins. . . ."

Mark 2.28: ". . . so the Son of Man is lord even of the sabbath."

I have put the Markan sayings last because I believe that these
are in a special category as I hope to make clear in a moment. The
discussion of this group of sayings is in a very interesting state at
this time because we have had two very different viewpoints expressed with regard to them by Eduard Schweizer and H. E. Tödt.

Eduard Schweizer's view, in contrast to the view of Bultmann
which Tödt accepted,[14] is that all three of the traditional groups
of Son of Man sayings[15] have a genuine core. In the "suffering"
group the authentic reference is to Jesus' being "handed over"; in
the "present" group it is to humility; and in the apocalyptic group
it is to exaltation rather than a "coming," as is usually argued.
Hence, the apocalyptic Son of Man sayings do not have an added
status over the others simply because they have a genuine core for
their origin. Rather, all three support the probability "that Jesus

14. It is one of the weaknesses of Tödt's work that he accepts the Bultmann position as a starting point for his own research rather than sub-
jecting it to the same kind of critical investigation that he gives to
other views.

15. This traditional division is usually ascribed to Bultmann, whose influence is certainly responsible for its widespread acceptance in German
language work. It appears for the first time in English, however, in 1920,
in Foakes, Jackson, and Lake, *Beginnings of Christianity* I, pp. 368–380.

spoke of himself as the Son of Man who was to be humiliated and rejected by men, yet exalted by God."[16] There is a two-fold preparation for this in Judaism. On the one hand there is the concept of the exaltation of the Son of Man found in 1 Enoch 70–71, and on the other there is "the pattern of the suffering righteous finally exalted by God as described in Psalm 22 and particularly in Wisdom 2–5."[17] Jesus himself "adopted the term *Son of Man* just because it is an ambiguous term, revealing as well as hiding."[18]

There are at least three things which must be said in criticism of this view. In the first place it is impossible to demonstrate the core of authenticity in each of the three groups of sayings to which Schweizer appealed, as Vielhauer shows in an extensive and carefully documented response to Schweizer.[19] Then, secondly, this *Vorbild* of the suffering righteous who would be exalted as Son of Man is difficult to document. True, ancient Judaism expected the suffering righteous to be rewarded—after all they believed in God! —but that the concept existed in quite the concrete form Schweizer must assume is questionable. Then thirdly—this is the criticism which I would stress—too many of the factors to which Schweizer appeals are explicable in terms of demonstrable Christian activity. The exaltation motif is a product of Christian exegetical reflection upon the fate of Jesus, as the same motif in 1 Enoch is the result of reflection upon the translation of Enoch; the "handed over" or "delivered up" (*paradidonai*) traditions are well-documented traditions resulting from the Christian apologetic for, and soteriological reflection upon, the cross, as I shall argue later; and the group of sayings with a present reference is a group of sayings with disparate origins whose present form, and in some cases whose very existence, is dependent upon Christian reflection on the ministry of Jesus, as I shall proceed to argue against Tödt. Schweizer's view is therefore an interesting *Neuheit* in the discussion, but it is ultimately untenable.

16. Schweizer, "The Son of Man," *JBL* 79 (1960), pp. 129–130.
17. Ibid., p. 128.
18. Ibid.
19. Vielhauer, "Jesus und der Menschensohn," *ZTK* 60 (1963), pp. 153–170.

Tödt's view[20] is very different, but equally interesting and, I shall maintain, equally untenable! He defines these sayings as "the sayings concerning the Son of Man's activity on earth" and treats them as belonging to a group which has a unity of emphasis upon the *exousia* (authority) of Jesus. Each saying, he argues, exhibits the *exousia* of the Son of Man; "this designation applies to Jesus acting in his sovereignty";[21] in these sayings "the name . . . designates Jesus in his specific sovereign activity by reason of his mission."[22] This is true of Luke 7:34 par., where Jesus "acts with supreme authority when bestowing table-fellowship on tax collectors and sinners,"[23] of Luke 12:10 par., which states "that opposition to Jesus' claim to authority can be forgiven,"[24] and even of Luke 9:58 par. where "the very one who summons men to full authority is the same whom this generation refuses to receive, thus depriving him of a home."[25] It is also true of Mark 2:10 and 2:28, and of Mark 10:45 which "is a real bridge between the kerygma of the passion and the sayings about the Son of Man's acting on earth with full authority."[26]

My arguments against Tödt on this point will be developed in the course of my discussion of the sayings themselves and they will follow a twofold line of attack. I shall be concerned to deny both the unity of this group of sayings and also the existence of the common emphasis upon the *exousia* of the earthly Jesus. So far as the unity of this group is concerned, Vielhauer has pointed out,[27] for example, how much violence Tödt has to do to the saying about the Son of Man having no place to lay his head to bring it into conformity with his pattern, and I shall argue that what we have here is a group of sayings of quite disparate origins which never achieves the unity which Tödt envisages. Then, secondly, the aura of *exousia* about these sayings is actually true only for Mark

20. Tödt, *Son of Man*, pp. 113–140.
21. Ibid., p. 116.
22. Ibid., p. 117.
23. Ibid., p. 115.
24. Ibid., p. 119.
25. Ibid., p. 122.
26. Ibid., p. 138.
27. Vielhauer, "Jesus und der Menschensohn," *ZTK* 60 (1963), p. 163.

2:10 and 2:28 and here it is due to Mark's preservation (or creation) and use of these sayings. Tödt really interprets the Q sayings in light of the Markan ones, but this is to underestimate the creative use being made by Mark of references to the Son of Man and his activity in the present.

Let me turn, then, to the question of the origins of these sayings with a present reference, origins which I see ultimately as disparate. To begin with Luke 7:34 and its parallel in Matt. 11:19, the interpretation of the Parable of the Children in the Marketplace, I myself have previously argued for the authenticity of this interpretation, that is, for its going back to Jesus himself,[28] and subsequent reinvestigation in preparation for this paper has not led me to any modification of this opinion. I am still convinced that the interpretation of the parable does go back to Jesus and that in the original interpretation of the parable, Son of Man was used by Jesus to designate himself. This usage is in accordance with the Aramaic idiom pointed out so strongly by Matthew Black and Geza Vermés.[29]

It is only when the saying is taken up into the Q tradition that the Son of Man reference comes to have the kind of formal christological ring that it now has. Originally it was simply an idiomatic self-designation of the speaker in contrast to another person, the idiom known to us from the rabbis, but in the hands of the editor or editors of the Q tradition it becomes something different. We have to recognize—and here I am wholly at one with Tödt who first convinced me of this point—that the Q tradition has a marked interest in the Son of Man. It was formed under the impetus of the expectation of the coming of Jesus as Son of Man, and it built up its collection of teachings of Jesus or teachings by prophets in the name of Jesus as a body of material which men could learn and follow in preparation for that coming. This is the genius of the Q material, and its link with the teachings of the historical Jesus is

28. See my *Rediscovering*, pp. 119–121.
29. Matthew Black, "The 'Son of Man' in the Teaching of Jesus," *Expository Times* 60 (1948/49), 32–36; Geza Vermés, "The Use of *Bar Nash/Bar Nasha* in Jewish Aramaic" (see above note 6).

possible because Jesus himself had proclaimed the coming of the Kingdom of God. At any rate, part of his teaching could be and no doubt was interpreted as preparing men for that coming. It clearly is the case that the Q tradition does reuse the teaching of Jesus and in so doing necessarily comes to reflect upon his ministry as the ministry of the one who is come as Son of Man. It seems to me, however, that Tödt goes too far in his attempt to show that in each of the sayings which are then produced in this way the authority of the future Son of Man is already to be seen. This really comes about only in Mark and then there are special reasons for it. What happens in Q is that the tradition reflects upon the ministry of Jesus as the ministry of the one who was Son of Man designate, the ministry of the one who was identical with the Son of Man, and hence begins to modify certain sayings which were products of that ministry or which now can be fitted into it, or to produce sayings which embody this reflection. So in the case of the saying which concerns us immediately, Luke 7:34 par., we have the idiomatic Son of Man as a self designation in this kind of a context transformed into a formal designation of Jesus as Son of Man, because, for the community transmitting this saying and meditating upon it, the Jesus who spoke of himself in this way is the Son of Man to come.

Luke 12:10 is a product of this reflection upon the ministry of Jesus as having been the ministry of the Son of Man, but here there is a further development. Not only does the community reflect upon the past ministry of Jesus and prepare itself for his future coming as Son of Man, it also begins to seek to understand its own interim present. So in this saying there is now a third epoch presupposed, namely, that of the ministry of the spirit in the present. The community is conscious that it possesses the spirit, it prophesies by this spirit, it transmits, reinterprets, and creates teaching of Jesus as Son of Man by this spirit, it challenges its fellow Jews by the authority of this spirit, and so on. In reflecting upon the ministry of Jesus in the past it has come to see that this ministry was essentially proleptic and the decisions made in this ministry not absolutely final. In the present there is time for change of heart before the whole will be ratified at the coming of the Son of Man. So a saying such as this is produced[30] to emphasize that a decision made against Jesus in his first ministry as Son of Man could now be changed in response to the challenge of the ministry of the spirit, but this was indeed the last opportunity, since the immediate and interim ministry of the spirit was shortly to be brought to a close by the coming of Jesus as Son of Man.

The saying Luke 9:58 does not seem to me to have any reflection of authority whatsoever. It has no real theological point, and I am at one with those who regard the origin of this saying as a popular proverb contrasting the lot of man as man in an economically depressed age with the blithe condition of the denizens of the animal kingdom.[31] In all probability here the original use of Son of Man was simply an idiom for man in general in contrast to the birds and beasts. It has come into the tradition in connection with Jesus simply because it could be used, once Son of Man had become a formal designation for Jesus, to express something of the consequences and circumstances of his ministry. When we consider the suffering sayings in our next section, we shall see that Son of Man is used to reflect upon the ministry of Jesus as necessarily ending in the passion. This makes the saying suitable to use in

---

30. It may be that this saying is produced by modifying an earlier saying such as the one now found in Mark 3:28–29. T. W. Manson (*Sayings of Jesus* [1949], 110) argued strongly that this form of the saying was earlier than the Q version (a view as old as Wellhausen) and that it was authentic. Fuller (*Foundations*, p. 125) follows Manson here and I myself am inclined also to do so. The saying in a form approximating to the Markan (allowing for ecclesiastical influence in verse 29) has a strong claim to authenticity: it stands at the beginning of a tradition (the Q version being derived from it); it has characteristics of Jesus' manner of speech (the *amēn legō hymīn*). "Its meaning is that the one unforgivable sin is to reject Jesus' eschatological message" (Fuller) and this coheres with a major emphasis of the message of the parables. If this is an authentic saying then we have here a further instance of the introduction of Son of Man by the church into such a saying. But note that Higgins (*Jesus*, pp. 127–132) argues strongly for the priority of the Q version and for the fact that this version comes from the church: "a pronouncement which arose in the early church in order to meet a current problem—Jewish opposition to the rejection of the church's offer of the Gospel—has been given a concrete situation in the life of Jesus himself" (Higgins, p. 130).

31. Vielhauer, "Jesus der Menschensohn," *ZTK* 60 (1963): *"Bultmanns Vermutung (ist) erneut zu erwägen."*

connection with Jesus although even then the application is somewhat mechanical.[32]

Luke 6:22 need not delay us for a moment; quite obviously,
once there was this identification of Jesus as Son of Man in the
tradition, then there could be a variety of usage in sayings between
the first personal pronoun and the Son of Man. Such variety is to be
found in the eschatological judgment pronouncements, in the eschatological correlatives when we get to John, and here in this
variation between "for my sake" and "for the Son of Man's sake."
These variations have no particular theological significance; they
are simply testimony to the complete identification of Jesus as Son
of Man and the consequent linguistic possibilities within the tradition.

The three sayings—Matt. 13:37, Mark 10:45, and Luke
19:10—are also a product of reflection upon the ministry of Jesus
or the ministry of the Son of Man. These sayings are evidence that
the church did indeed reflect upon the ministry of the Son of Man
in the past as well as anticipate his coming in the future. Each of
them offers us a particular evangelist's understanding of the ministry of Jesus, and Matt. 13:37 and Mark 10:45 may be products of
the evangelists themselves. But Tödt argues[33] strongly and surely
correctly that Luke 19:10 is traditional, and it is therefore evidence for the existence of this form of saying in the tradition of the
church.

Until one comes to Mark, then, the Son of Man sayings with a
present reference appear to have a variety of origins: a change
from an idiom preserved in a genuine saying of Jesus, reflection
upon the ministry of Jesus as the ministry of the Son of Man,
reflection upon the ministry of Jesus and the ministry of the spirit
in the interim period between that ministry and the coming judg-

---

32. It is somewhat mechanical because the saying does not actually represent the circumstances of the passion in any way. But it reflects the
actual circumstances of the life of Jesus, so far as the tradition knows
them, not at all (Vielhauer, *ZTK* 60 [1963], p. 162), which makes it
impossible to accept as a saying from Jesus himself. So the best explanation remains: a popular proverb somewhat mechanically applied
to Jesus in the tradition because it uses the Son of Man.

33. Tödt, *Son of Man*, pp. 133–135.

ment of the Son of Man, reflection on the significance of the ministry of Jesus altogether, and results of the complete identification of Jesus as Son of Man with its consequent linguistic possibilities. There is nothing here, I would argue, to justify the claim that we have a well-integrated and definite group of sayings reflecting a common emphasis. Nor is there here any consistent reference to the authority of Jesus. When we come to Mark this changes, for Mark 2:10 (the claim of the Son of Man having authority on earth to forgive sins) and Mark 2:28 (the similar claim that the Son of Man is lord of the Sabbath) clearly exhibit the *exousia* of the earthly Jesus as Son of Man as Tödt claims they do. But there is strong evidence, to which I now turn, that this is a feature of the Markan theology, rather than a feature of the Q tradition, or of early Christianity in general.

It is an important but little noted fact that the Greek word *exousia* is never used of the earthly Jesus in the synoptic tradition except in Mark or in dependence on Mark! There are only two possible exceptions to this, Matt. 28:18 and Luke 12:5. But in Matt. 28:18 (the Great Commission) it is the Risen Lord to whom "all *exousia* in heaven and earth has been given," and in Luke 12:15, it is either God or Jesus as apocalyptic Son of Man who has *exousia* "to cast into hell." So these two references are not to the earthly Jesus. In other words, it is to Mark—not to Q, not to M, not to L, but to Mark—that we owe the use of *exousia* in connection with the earthly Jesus. In light of this fact Tödt's confident use of *exousia* in connection with sayings from both Mark and Q (p. 139) or from Q alone (p. 124) must be questioned. In this specific respect, this group of sayings is not a unity and one may not, therefore, interpret the Q sayings in light of Mark 2:10 and 2:28, which is what Tödt in effect does.

We have come to the point at which it would be natural to go on to discuss the role of Mark 2:10 and 2:28 in the Markan theology, but Mark is so important in the Son of Man traditions altogether that we must leave that for the moment and turn instead to the third category into which Son of Man sayings are traditionally divided.

THE SUFFERING SON OF MAN SAYINGS

It has been frequently observed that the suffering Son of Man sayings, now found at Mark 8:31, 9:31, and 10:33–34, are to be found only in Mark and in dependence upon Mark. Further, it is widely recognized that in their present form they are a creation of Mark. But Mark has not created them *ex nihilo*. There is in fact a rather complex tradition reaching back into the earliest days of Christian apologetic upon which Mark has drawn in the fashioning of the sayings. The Christian church has reflected upon the passion of Jesus deeply and extensively, and for three different although not wholly distinct reasons. First of all, there is the necessity for Christians themselves, for the most part Jews by birth and training, to come to terms with the fact that the one in whom they are coming to believe as Lord, Son of Man, and Messiah had been crucified. Secondly, there is the necessity for making an apologetic over against Judaism with regard to the crucified Messiah. Thirdly, chronologically later than either of the first two, there is the development of a soteriological significance attaching to the cross and the exploration of its meaning for faith. Fortunately we now know a great deal about these various processes, in part because of the work of Tödt and Hahn on the traditions using *paradidonai*,[34] in part because of the work of Barnabas Lindars on the use of the Old Testament in this connection.[35] Many others have, of course, contributed to our knowledge here, but these are the two strands of the work done in the field which concern me most at the moment.

The work on the traditions using *paradidonai* done in turn by Tödt and Hahn has established the fact that there are two distinct usages of this verb in connection with the passion of Jesus. First, we have what I shall call the apologetic *paradidonai* tradition. Here, we have the verb being used in connection with the passion, often with a further reference to the persons, etc., to whom Jesus was delivered up. When a title is used it is Son of Man, and the

34. Ibid., pp. 156–161; Hahn, *Titles*, pp. 37–42.
35. Barnabas Lindars, *New Testament Apologetic* (1961), especially chapters III and IV.

stress of the whole is upon the apocalyptic and scriptural necessity for the passion. This tradition is oriented toward apologetic both within the church and outside it. Examples of this tradition are Mark 14:21 ("For the Son of Man goes as it is written of him, but woe to that man by whom the Son of Man *paradidotai*") and 14:41 (". . . the hour is come, the Son of Man *paradidotai* into the hands of sinners"), both certainly pre-Markan. Then, secondly, we have what I shall call the soteriological *paradidonai* tradition. Here the verb is used with a phrase recalling Isaiah 53, the title is never Son of Man, and the stress is upon the soteriological significance of the passion. Examples are: Rom. 4:25, where Jesus, our Lord, was "delivered up for our trespasses and raised for our justification"; Rom. 8:32, where God's own Son was "delivered up for us all"; Gal. 2:20, where the Son of God "loved me and gave himself up for me"; and Eph. 5:2, where Christ loved us and gave himself for us. These two traditions are distinct and must be kept distinct in our thinking. The apologetic one seems to belong in the Palestinian area of traditions; it may not originally have been in Greek and it certainly echoes Palestinian ways of thinking throughout. The soteriological tradition, however, is thoroughly Greek. Tödt has convinced me that this tradition was in Greek from the very beginning, that it used Isaiah 53 in Greek, that it belongs in the area of Hellenistic Christianity. Not that Palestinian Christianity did not meditate ultimately upon the soteriological significance of the cross, but it came to it rather more slowly and when it did come to it, it seems to me to have come to it very largely in a Passover setting.[36]

Another traditional element reflected in the passion predictions is the use of Psalm 118 in a Christian exegetical tradition. Lindars has shown[37] that there is a tradition which uses Psalm 118 in a pesher-like manner to interpret the resurrection and then in the service of apologetic and perhaps also in that of a soteriology. It is

36. I am inclined to support the suggestion put forward by Fuller (*Foundations*, p. 119 and the further reference given there) that the Palestinian church's soteriological understanding of the cross developed in a Passover setting, although not, I think, as early as 31 C.E.

37. Lindars, *New Testament Apologetic*, pp. 81, 169–176.

as Ps. 118:22 is used in this tradition that "to be rejected" (*apodokimazō*) and "to be treated with contempt" (*exoudeneō*) come to be used as synonyms, as they are in Acts 4:11, Mark 8:31, 9:12, and 12:10–11, all of which must be held to reflect this Christian exegetical tradition.[38]

I shall not stay to discuss other traditional elements in the material used by Mark in his passion predictions. It is enough for my purpose to claim that he inherits the two *paradidonai* traditions isolated by Tödt and Hahn and the exegetical-apologetic tradition illuminated by Lindars. That he knows the Palestinian apologetic *paradidonai* tradition using Son of Man is clear from Mark 14:32, 35, 40, and 42 which K. G. Kuhn isolated as a pre-Markan story with Gethsemane as its locale,[39] and which reflects this tradition. The predictions themselves do not necessarily reflect the Hellenistic soteriological *paradidonai* traditions using Isaiah 53, but that Mark knows this tradition is clear from 10:45b which, I would argue, reflects this tradition, and which certainly alludes to Isaiah 53. So I am fully prepared to follow, in general terms, Tödt's reconstruction of the process by means of which Mark has composed the passion predictions on the basis of traditional material and in a paper of this compass I need not to stay to discuss the details. The particular emphases I would want to make will become evident as I discuss the whole subject of the use of Son of Man by Mark.

THE USE OF SON OF MAN BY MARK

It is my contention that the evangelist Mark is the major figure in the creative use of Son of Man traditions in the New Testament period. To him we owe the general picture we have from the Gospels that Son of Man is Jesus' own favorite self designation

---

38. Lindars is inclined to see *exoudeneō* as an allusion to Isa. 55:3 (p. 81) and hence to find a soteriological element in this particular tradition. I would see the verb as coming from Psalm 22 (LXX 21):7, 25, and the emphasis as therefore apologetic throughout.
39. K. G. Kuhn, "Jesus in Gethsemane," *EvTH* 12 (1952/53), pp. 260–285.

and that Jesus used it to teach his disciples to understand both the true nature of his messiahship, as including suffering and glory, and the true nature of Christian discipleship, as the way to glory through suffering. Because of the Gospel of Mark we get the impression that this is what Jesus does, but this is actually what Mark does, for recent research has shown that a major purpose in the writing of the Markan Gospel is a christological purpose;[40] it was the purpose of the evangelist to teach the Christians of his day a true Christology in place of the false Christology which he felt they were in danger of accepting. The method he chooses is that of a most carefully constructed narrative in which the false Christology is put on the lips of the disciples and the true Christology on the lips of Jesus. Moreover, for reasons that I shall make clear in a moment, Mark chooses to represent the true Christology by using the term *Son of Man*; in effect, he uses Son of Man to give content to the idea of Jesus as Son of God. That for Mark Son of God is the all-important title can be seen from the presence of this title in the superscription to the Gospel and in the climactic christological statement of the Centurion at Calvary. In between these two occurrences of Son of God are references to Son of Man which serve to give content to the conception of Jesus as Son of God. These references are very carefully arranged, as we shall see.

Before turning to the actual details of the Markan presentation, we must ask ourselves again what it is that Mark inherits from the tradition. From the foregoing discussion it will have become clear that I regard Mark as inheriting three traditional uses of Son of Man, and one other tradition related to the last of these three. First of all, he inherits the apocalyptic Son of Man sayings which I have described as originating in an exegesis of the Old Testament and spreading through various ecclesiastical traditions such as the eschatological judgment pronouncement tradition, the eschatological correlative, and the apocalyptic promises. Then, secondly, he inherits the tendency from the tradition to reflect upon the ministry

40. Johannes Schreiber, "Die Christologie des Markusevangeliums," *ZTK* 58 (1961), pp. 154–183; J. B. Tyson, "The Blindness of the Disciples in Mark," *JBL* 80 (1961), pp. 261–268; T. J. Weeden, *Mark—Traditions in Conflict* (1971).

of Jesus as the ministry of the Son of Man designate and eventually of the Son of Man himself. This tendency has produced those sayings which are traditionally described as having a present reference and in my view are of disparate origins. Then, finally, he inherits and unites two traditions using *paradidonai* in connection with the passion of Jesus: what I have called the apologetic *paradidonai* tradition which uses Son of Man and the soteriological *paradidonai* tradition which does not.

If this contention is correct, then the specifically Markan uses of Son of Man are concentrated in the sequence of references which begins with 2:10 and ends with 10:45. The first Son of Man reference in the Gospel is 2:10 and the ones after 10:45 are simply embedded in traditional material and allowed to stand by Mark; 13:26 is an apocalyptic promise; 14:21, 41 are from the apologetic *paradidonai* tradition; 14:62 from the Christian exegetical tradition which began it all; and all are in material where Markan redactional and compositional activity is at a minimum. This is an observation upon which I would put a good deal of weight. I am very much concerned to argue that the Markan theological use of Son of Man becomes evident if we simply regard 13:26, 14:21, 14:41, and 14:62 as traditional sayings allowed to stand in material taken over by Mark and then concentrate on the sequence of references from 2:10 to 10:45. The one possible break in this sequence is Mark 9:12b which may well be a traditional reference preserved by Mark because it stood in his source. But it fits into the particular emphasis which concerns Mark at that point, which is why he allowed it to stand.

Let us then proceed to look at those places which I consider to represent the Markan theological use of Son of Man, turning first to the two references to the Son of Man's authority in 2:10 and 2:28, in the former to forgive sins and in the latter to abrogate the Sabbath law. As I said earlier, there can be no doubt that these sayings are a full-scale presentation of the authority of Jesus as Son of Man being exercised in his earthly ministry, and it is because he links these sayings so closely with those which have a present reference that Tödt is able to argue for the whole group exhibiting the authority of the Son of Man. But if we isolate these sayings from the remainder of the group, then we can see that the emphasis upon the authority is a particularly Markan emphasis. No other saying of this group sets off the authority of Jesus as do these sayings, partly because no other sayings of the group are set in a context such as this one and partly because no other sayings have quite the content that these have. Mark has a whole section at the beginning of his Gospel which stresses the authority of Jesus as he enters upon his ministry. This section is from 1:16–3:6; here we have Jesus calling disciples, healing the sick, and teaching with authority—in other words exercising his authority in every possible kind of way—and here we have Jesus also involved in controversy with his Jewish contemporaries. This section has been carefully composed by Mark in order to exhibit the authority of Jesus. This would be true even if he is using a cycle of traditional controversy stories, because 3:6 is certainly Markan and the whole section 2:1–3:6 moves carefully to this climax.[41] Tödt argues that Mark inherited the Son of Man sayings as part of his tradition and simply allowed them to stand,[42] but the fact to which I called attention earlier, namely, that *exousia* is used of the earthly Jesus in the synoptic tradition only in Mark or in dependence upon Mark, surely makes a difference at this point. In a paper of this compass I cannot stay to discuss the actual composition of these sayings, but the facts of life with regard to this use of *exousia* must be held to prove that whether Mark has created them, redacted them, or simply preserved them, they represent a characteristic emphasis of the Markan theology.

After 2:28 the next reference to Son of Man in Mark is to be found in the Caesarea Philippi pericope and it would be universally agreed that this pericope does serve in the Markan purpose as the watershed of the Gospel. It specifically introduces the notion of the suffering element into the Son of Man Christology, although in typically Markan style there has been a preparation for this even at the end of the section on the authority of Jesus, i.e., at

41. Martin Dibelius, *From Tradition to Gospel*, p. 219.
42. Tödt, *Son of Man*, p. 132.

3:6. It cannot be accidental that we have only those two climactic authority references to the Son of Man in the section on Jesus' authority and then no further reference to Son of Man at all until we come to Caesarea Philippi, where we find both the authority of the Son of Man in 8:38[43] and the suffering of the Son of Man in 8:31. What we have in fact is a carefully arranged sequence of references: 2:10 and 2:28, the Son of Man's authority on earth; 8:31, the Son of Man's necessary suffering; and 8:38, the Son of Man's authority in judgment. Once we learn to think of Mark consciously composing his material—as we must—we can recognize the significance of this for his purpose. His purpose is to fill the concept of Jesus as Son of God with the notion of both authority and suffering, and his use of Son of Man is the means by which he chooses to do this. So Son of Man occurs again in the very carefully composed section 8:27–10:52 in which, as is well known, we have the threefold emphasis upon the suffering Son of Man followed in each instance by misunderstanding and teaching. The pattern is therefore earthly authority, suffering, and final authority, and then the development of the suffering theme.

The suffering Son of Man sayings in their present form are again a Markan production, although he is working with material he has inherited from the tradition, as I indicated earlier. The climax to the section 8:27–10:52, which we must all recognize is intended as the introduction to an interpretation of the passion and for this reason is the vehicle for the suffering sayings, is found in Mark 10:45. Here we move from prediction of the passion to reflection upon its soteriological significance; we are moving from the idea of apocalyptic and scriptural necessity to the idea of soteriological significance, and we are in fact at the heart of the Markan theological enterprise.

Mark 10:45 is unique among the Son of Man sayings, although it shares with Matthew 13:37 and Luke 19:10 the tendency to reflect on the ministry of Jesus. In the compass of this paper I

---

43. 8:38 does not use *exousia* but does express the apocalyptic authority of the Son of Man at the judgment. That this is *exousia* can be seen from Luke 12:5 which uses the word in this context.

cannot discuss the vexed question as to whether it is, wholly or in part, a Markan production. So far as the purpose of this paper is concerned it does not matter, for whether Mark is composing, redacting, or simply using the saying, its position as the climax of the section 8:27–10:52 alone guarantees its immense importance for the Markan theology. 10:45 is the climax of the Markan presentation of Jesus as Son of Man. We have moved from earthly authority through the necessity of suffering to apocalyptic authority; and we have moved also from the necessity for the passion to the soteriological significance of the cross. All this is bound together into a unity for Mark because it can all be expressed in terms of Son of Man, which must be the reason for the central place he gives to the title in his Gospel.

Son of Man is the natural title for Mark to use in this way because it was comparatively unused in the tradition before him and was not a confessional title. Thus, there was no weight of traditional use to predetermine the understanding of his audience. Then, such uses as there were all tended to fit into the pattern he is concerned to establish: a deliberate blend of earthly authority, the necessity of suffering, apocalyptic authority, and soteriological significance. The "present" use could become *exousia*; the apocalyptic use was already there; the *paradidonai* traditions foreshadowed the suffering use; and the reflection upon the ministry of Jesus as that of the Son of Man could lead (or had led) to the soteriology of 10:45. For these reasons, I suggest, Mark chose to use Son of Man as the vehicle for the presentation of the true understanding of Jesus as Son of God which it is the purpose of his Gospel to present.

The remaining Son of Man sayings in Mark—the apocalyptic promise in 13:26, the two references to the "delivering up" of the Son of Man in 14:21, 41 and the deposit from a Christian exegetical tradition used in 14:62—are, I would maintain, traditional references which Mark inherits and allows to stand in his material. They do not disturb his purpose, but they are not so essential to him as is the sequence of Son of Man sayings which reaches a climax in 10:45. So he allows them to stand without serious modification. We must recognize the hand of Mark most actively at work in what I regard as a deliberately and carefully planned, and even composed, sequence of sayings beginning in 2:10 and climaxing in 10:45. Here we have the deliberate impression being created that Jesus taught this as the innermost secret of his self-understanding. This we have because here Mark is choosing to put the true Christology upon the lips of Jesus, having put the false one upon the lips of the disciples, and choosing to do this by the use of Son of Man because only Son of Man lends itself to the necessary combination of theological motifs.

POSTSCRIPT

This remains the most comprehensive statement of my views on the Son of Man sayings in the synoptic tradition, that is, in the traditional material as it existed prior to the writing of the Synoptic Gospels. What is significant about the essay to me in retrospect is the fact that even though I set out to discuss the Son of Man sayings in the synoptic tradition I found myself inevitably discussing the Son of Man in a synoptic gospel, namely, the Gospel of Mark. I say "inevitably discussing" because it is my conclusion that the evangelist Mark is so overwhelming a figure in the development of the Christology associated with Son of Man in the New Testament that wherever one begins it is not long before one is talking about him. There is to me an aura of inevitability about the fact that I began by investigating the Son of Man in the synoptic tradition and ended by attempting an interpretation of the Gospel of Mark.

In connection with the interpretation of the Gospel of Mark, I must confess that I am somewhat embarrassed today to reprint the paragraph which begins: "If this contention is correct, then the specifically Markan uses of Son of Man are concentrated in the sequence of references which begins with 2:10 and ends with 10:45." Today it is obvious to me that the references after 10:45 are every bit as representative of Mark's literary activity and of his overall theological purpose as are those before that saying. I take up this matter in some detail in the essay which concludes this volume.

CHAPTER VI

The Creative Use of the
Son of Man Traditions by Mark

It is the contention of this article that the evangelist Mark is a major figure in the creative use of Son of Man traditions in the New Testament period. To him we owe the general picture we have from the Gospels that "Son of Man" is Jesus' favorite self-designation and that Jesus used it to teach his disciples to understand both the true nature of his messiahship as including suffering and glory, and the true nature of Christian discipleship as the way to glory through suffering. Because of the Gospel of Mark, we get the impression that this is what Jesus does, but this is actually what Mark does, for recent research has shown that a major purpose in the writing of the Markan Gospel is christological.[1] It was the purpose of the evangelist to teach the Christians of his day a true Christology in place of the false Christology that he felt they were in danger of accepting. The method he chooses is that of a most carefully constructed narrative in which the false Christology is put on the lips of the disciples and the true Christology is put on the lips of Jesus.

The most important christological title in the Gospel is Son of

---

1. Schreiber, "Die Christologie des Markusevangeliums," *ZTK* 58 (1961), pp. 154–183; J. B. Tyson, "The Blindness of the Disciples in Mark," *JBL* 80 (1961), pp. 261–268; Ulrich Luz, "Das Geheimnismotiv und die markinische Christologie," *ZNW* 56 (1965), 9–30; Philip Vielhauer, "Erwägungen zur Christologie des Markusevangeliums," in Vielhauer, *Aufsätze zum Neuen Testament* (1965), pp. 199–214 (=*Zeit und Geschichte. Dankesgabe an Rudolf Bultmann*, pp. 155–169); T. J. Weeden, *Mark—Traditions in Conflict* (1971).

God. That this is the case can be seen from the fact that it stands in the superscription to the Gospel and it is used in the climactic christological statement of the Centurion at Calvary. Moreover, as Vielhauer has pointed out,[2] it is the title which Mark uses in those narratives where it is clear that he sees something happening that is crucial for an understanding of Jesus and where his own interpretative work is at a maximum: the baptism (1:11), the transfiguration (9:7), and the confession by the Centurion already mentioned (15:39). Occurring as it does, therefore, in the superscription, the confessional climax, and the two crucial episodes of baptism and transfiguration, Son of God may justly be described as the most important title for Mark, and the basic christological structure of his Gospel may be held to be built upon these references.

The use of Son of Man in Mark is crucial to an understanding of the nature of that divine sonship as Mark understands it. In effect, he uses Son of Man to interpret and to give content to the conception of Jesus as Son of God. One may note, for example, the juxtaposition of the two titles throughout the Gospel. In 3:11, a Markan summary emphasizes that Jesus exercises his authority on earth as Son of God; in 2:10 and 2:28, Mark stresses his *exousia* as Son of Man. Chapter 8, verse 38 (Caesarea Philippi) is a statement of the apocalyptic authority of Jesus as Son of Man; seven verses later in a narrative carefully linked to that by a time reference, the voice addresses the transfigured Jesus as "my beloved Son." The High Priest asks Jesus whether he is "the Son of the Blessed"; the reply is in terms of the Son of Man (14:61–62). For Mark, the meaning of Son of God is to be expressed in terms of a use of Son of Man. Since, as I have already claimed, it is his literary device to put that true Christology on the lips of Jesus, he rigidly restricts that title to those lips.

In order to arrive at an understanding of the Markan use of Son of Man, we have to be able to distinguish between traditional uses allowed to stand in inherited material and special Markan redaction or composition. The former will tell us something of the

2. Veilhauer, "Erwägungen zur Christologie des Markusevangeliums."

authority in 2:10 and 2:28, in the former to forgive sins and in the latter to abrogate the Sabbath law. These sayings are a full-scale presentation of the authority of Jesus as Son of Man being exercised in his earthly ministry. With other sayings in the tradition (Matt. 11:19 par., 12:32 par.) they share the characteristic of speaking of the work of the Son of Man in the present, and Tödt has argued that all of these sayings reflect the *exousia* of the Son of Man,[7] that Mark 2:10 and 2:28 are in fact sayings inherited by Mark from the tradition. But I would argue that the emphasis upon *exousia* so characteristic of Mark 2:10 (where the word is actually found) and 2:28 (where it is certainly implied) is a Markan emphasis. One can see this, in the first place, from the compositional activity of the evangelist in the section of the Gospel in which these sayings are set. This section is from 1:16 to 3:6; here we have Jesus calling disciples, healing the sick, and teaching with authority—exercising his authority in every possible kind of way—and here we also have Jesus involved in controversy with his Jewish contemporaries. This section has been carefully composed by Mark in order to exhibit the authority of Jesus. This would be true even if he is using a cycle of traditional controversy stories, because 3:6 is certainly Markan and the whole section of 2:1 to 3:6 moves carefully to this climax.[8] Then, in the second place, it is an important but little noted fact that the Greek word *exousia* is never used of the earthly Jesus in the synoptic tradition except in Mark or in dependence upon Mark! The tradition is moving toward this, because in the Q story of the Centurion's servant (Matt. 8:5–13 par.) *exousia* is used by the Centurion both in reference to himself and, by implication, in reference to Jesus (Matt. 8:9 par.), but never before Mark does the tradition actually reach the point of using the word. It is to Mark that we owe the actual use of *exousia* in connection with the earthly Jesus.[9] It may be that in

---

7. H. E. Tödt, *Son of Man*, pp. 113–140.
8. Martin Dibelius, *From Tradition to Gospel*, p. 219.
9. The only two possible exceptions to this are Matt. 28:18 and Luke 12:5. But in Matt. 28:18 (the Great Commission), it is the Risen Lord to whom "all *exousia* in heaven and earth has been given," and in Luke 12:5 it is either God or Jesus as apocalyptic Son of Man who has *exousia* "to cast into hell." So these two references are not to the earthly Jesus.

this he is only taking the last step by making explicit something already implicit in the tradition before him, but nonetheless it is he who takes this step and who thereby establishes the emphasis as his own. In view of this, these two sayings (2:10 and 2:28) may not be regarded as representing a traditional use of Son of Man which Mark inherits and allows to stand in the material. Here we have to seek evidence of Mark's own theological motivation, and there can be no doubt as to what the evidence indicates. Mark intends both to stress the authority of Jesus and to claim that he exercised that authority as Son of Man. This is the first element in his Christology.

After 2:28, the next reference to Son of Man in Mark is to be found in the Caesarea Philippi pericope; it would be universally agreed that this pericope does serve in the Markan purpose as the watershed of the Gospel. It specifically introduces the notion of the suffering element into the Son of Man Christology. Although in typically Markan style, there has been a preparation for this even at the end of the section on the authority of Jesus, at 3:6. It cannot be accidental that we have only those two climactic authority references to the Son of Man in the section on Jesus' authority and then no further reference to Son of Man at all until we come to Caesarea Philippi, where we find both the authority of the Son of Man in 8:38 and the suffering of the Son of Man in 8:31. What we have, in fact, is a carefully arranged sequence of references: 2:10 and 2:28, the Son of Man's authority on earth; 8:31, the Son of Man's necessary suffering; and 8:38, the Son of Man's apocalyptic authority.

It will be most convenient to take first the saying about the apocalyptic authority of the Son of Man, chapter 8, verse 38. Here I would follow Käsemann and claim that this saying is a Markan redaction of a *Satz heiligen Rechtes* such as that now found in Luke 12:8–9.[10] Mark has produced it to serve as the first of the

10. Ernst Käsemann, "Sätze heiligen Rechtes im Neuen Testament," *NTS* 1 (1954/55), pp. 248–260 = *Exegetische Versuche und Besinnungen II*, pp. 69–82. (English, "Sentences of Holy Law in the New Testament," in Ernst Käsemann, *New Testament Questions of Today*, pp. 66–81). On this extremely important form-critical investigation, see my *Rediscovering*, pp. 22–23.

two sayings which climax his Caesarea Philippi narrative. It also serves his christological purpose by linking together the earthly and the apocalyptic authority of Jesus as Son of Man.

Mark 8:31 is the first of the three passion predictions: 8:31, 9:31, and 10:33–34. The history of the tradition lying behind these predictions is beyond our present capacity to unravel; we cannot know how much of them is traditional or how much is due to Markan redaction or composition. It is clear, for example, that the two traditional uses of Son of Man in connection with the passion I discussed earlier lie behind some part of these sayings. Other traditional motives can perhaps also be distinguished.[11] But the situation with the passion predictions is exactly the same as with the sayings concerning the Son of Man's authority in chapter 2 of the Gospel; it is universally recognized that the presence of the passion predictions in the synoptic tradition is due to Mark. Moreover, these predictions occur in a section of the Gospel, 8:27–10:52, which we must all recognize as being intended as the introduction to and interpretation of the passion, as offering us the Markan theology of the cross in all its intensity, and as being very carefully composed by Mark to serve this purpose.

Following in part the excellent analysis of this section by Tödt[12] but making some additions of my own, I would like to point out the following facts about this section of the Gospel. First of all, it is clearly divided into three parts by means of careful geographical references: 8:27: ". . . to the villages of Caesarea Philippi" (north of Galilee); 9:30: ". . . from there and passed through Galilee"; and 10:1: ". . . he left there and went to the region of Judea and beyond the Jordan" (i.e., toward Jerusalem). Each of these three divisions of the unit has its own passion prediction (8:31, 9:31, and 10:33–34); and the dramatic tension is heightened by the fact that the last one includes a specific reference to the Jerusalem toward which the group is moving as the locale of

11. The most recent discussion of this problem is Georg Strecker, "The Passion and Resurrection Predictions in Mark's Gospel," *Interpretation* 22 (1968), pp. 421–422.
12. Tödt, *Son of Man*, pp. 145–149.

the passion. Further, each passion prediction occurs in a contextual pattern which is constant throughout: there is always a prediction, a misunderstanding, and then teaching about discipleship. The first prediction is followed by the rebuke of Peter, the second by a reference to the disciples' misunderstanding and then by a dispute about greatness, the third with dramatic irony by the request of the sons of Zebedee. The three units of teaching on discipleship are to be found in 8:34 ff., 9:35 ff., and 10:38 ff. Each of these sections of teaching makes its own particular point. Put together, they represent the basic Markan understanding of the nature of Christian discipleship, and, moreover, they progress to a climax in 10:45. In the first section discipleship is defined in terms of preparedness to take up the cross, in the second as preparedness to be last and servant of all, and in the third servanthood is defined in terms of the Son of Man who "also came not to be served but to serve, and to give his life as a ransom for many." This arrangement of the material is very effective indeed, and it clearly represents a very strong element of redactional and compositional activity on the part of the evangelist.

Whatever may be the case, therefore, with regard to the element of Markan redaction or composition in the passion predictions themselves, the two elements to which I have called attention, namely, the fact that Mark is responsible for their presence in the synoptic tradition and that they are a key element in what is evidently a very carefully composed section of the Gospel, wholly justify us in treating them as reflecting the Markan theology.

Mark 10:45 must be considered together with the passion predictions, for, although this is unique among the Son of Man sayings, it is the climax to which the whole section of the Gospel in which the passion predictions are set clearly and carefully moves. Again, this is a saying where, for the moment, we are unable to determine the extent of the Markan redaction or composition. It shares with Matt. 13:37 and Luke 10:10 a tendency to reflect on the ministry of Jesus as that of the Son of Man, and it may be that it has been produced out of a creative interaction between a saying about service, such as the one now to be found in Luke 22:27, and the soteriological *paradidonai* tradition. Son of Man may then have been introduced into it either in response to a general tendency to move between the first personal pronoun and Son of Man—a tendency which is observable in the synoptic tradition—or it may have been introduced by Mark himself. But whatever may be the case with the composition of the saying, its climactic setting and function in this section of the Gospel alone guarantees its immense importance for the Markan theology. Mark 10:45 is the climax of the Markan presentation of Jesus as Son of Man. We have moved from earthly authority through the necessity of suffering to apocalyptic authority. We have moved also from the necessity for the passion to the soteriological significance of the cross.

It can be seen that there is a clear pattern to Mark's use of Son of Man. His overall purpose is to use the term to interpret and to give a correct content to the belief in Jesus as Son of God, and he begins therefore with a clear statement of the theme of Jesus' earthly authority as Son of God/Son of Man. Then he goes on to a first statement of the theme of the necessity for the suffering of the Son of Man. Then he sounds the note of apocalyptic authority before turning to his major development of the suffering theme. Finally, he reaches a climax in which the soteriological significance of the passion of the Son of Man is dramatically presented. He can unite these themes precisely because he can use Son of Man to state each one of them. Son of Man was in use before him in connection with the earthly ministry of Jesus; it remained for him to develop the emphasis upon *exousia*. Son of Man was being used in apocalyptic sayings before him; he could simply take such a saying and fit it into his pattern. Son of Man was to be found in connection with the passion before him; it remained for him to develop the passion predictions and the teaching about discipleship so firmly linked with them. Finally, an I-saying about service could (or had already) become a soteriological Son of Man saying.

I would claim that the Markan use of Son of Man reveals a threefold purpose: the necessity for combating a false understanding of Jesus as Son of God and replacing it by one which emphasized the necessity for suffering; the development of the theme that the necessity for suffering is laid also upon the disciples; and the understanding of that necessary suffering as the way to the salvation of mankind when accepted by Jesus and as the way to glory for the believer when accepted by him. All of this is held together by the use of Son of Man. This is not only the most creative moment in the use of Son of Man in the New Testament; it is also one of the most creative moments in the development of the theology of the New Testament altogether.

CHAPTER VII

The Use of *(Para)didonai*
in Connection with the Passion
of Jesus in the New Testament

In recent times there has been some discussion of the use of
(para)didonai in the New Testament in connection with the passion of Jesus. J. Jeremias in his *Theological Dictionary* article *pais
theou*[1] stated a position with regard to it and subsequently modi-
fied that position in a second, revised edition of the article. Both
H. E. Tödt in his *Son of Man in the Synoptic Tradition* and
Ferdinand Hahn in *The Titles of Jesus in Christology* have debated
the matter with Jeremias and one another. It is the purpose of this
article to take up a position in the light of this discussion and of
some further observations.

We may begin by simply listing the relevant texts and, following
a hint by Jeremias, listing them in three groups depending on the
use of the verb: (1) using *(para)didonai* in the active; (2) using
(para)didonai in the passive; (3) using *(para)didonai* in the active with a reflexive object.

(1) Using *(para)didonai* in the active:

Matt: 10:4: Judas Iscariot, who betrayed *(paradous)* him" [and
the very frequent similar references].

1. Walther Zimmerli and Joachim Jeremias, *The Servant of God* (1957;
rev. ed. 1965).

Mark 14:42: "See, my betrayer (*paradidous*) is at hand." [Cf. 14:41 in (2) below.]

Acts 3:13: ". . . Jesus, whom you delivered up (*paredōkate*) . . ."

Rom. 8:32: "He who did not spare his own Son but gave him up (*paredōken*) for (*hyper*) us all."

(2) Using *(para)didonai* in the passive:

Mark 9:31: "The Son of Man will be delivered (*paradidotai*) into the hands of men . . ."

Mark 10:33: ". . . the Son of Man will be delivered (*paradothēsetai*) to the chief priests . . ."

Mark 14:41: " . . . the Son of Man is betrayed (*paradidotai*) into the hands of sinners." [Cf. 14:42 in (1) above.]

[Matt. 26:2]: ". . . the Son of Man will be delivered up (*paradidotai*) to be crucified."

[Luke 24:7]: ". . . the Son of Man must be delivered (*paradothēnai*) into the hands of sinful men . . ."

1 Cor. 11:23: ". . . the Lord Jesus on the night when he was betrayed (*paredidoto*) . . ."

Rom. 4:25: "Jesus our Lord, who was put to death (*paredothē*) for our trespasses . . ."

There are two further texts which have to be brought into the discussion here because of their obvious relationship to Mark 9:31 and 10:33:

Mark 8:31: ". . . the Son of Man must suffer many things, and be rejected . . ."

Mark 9:12: ". . . how is it written of the Son of Man, that he should suffer many things and be treated with contempt?"

(3) Using *(para)didonai* in the active with a reflexive object:

Mark 10:45: "For the Son of Man also came . . . to give (*dounai*) his life as a ransom for (*anti*) many."

1 Tim. 2:6: ". . . the man Christ Jesus, who gave (*dous*) himself as a ransom for (*hyper*) all."

Titus 2:14: ". . . Jesus Christ, who gave (*edōken*) himself for (*hyper*) us . . ."

Gal. 1:4: ". . . our Lord Jesus Christ, who gave (*dontos*) himself for (*hyper*) our sins . . ."

Gal. 2:20: ". . . the Son of God, who loved me and gave (*paradontos*) himself for (*hyper*) me."

Eph. 5:2: ". . . as Christ loved us and gave himself up (*paredōken*) for (*hyper*) us."

Eph. 5:25: ". . . as Christ loved the church and gave himself up (*paredōken*) for (*hyper*) her."

There are two other texts which can be added at this point as relating to the use of *hyper*, if not to that of (*para*)*didonai*:

1 Cor. 15:3: ". . . Christ died for (*hyper*) our sins according to the scriptures . . ."

1 Cor. 11:24: "This is my body which is for (*hyper*) you."

[Cf. Mark 14:24:] "This is my blood of the covenant which is poured out for (*hyper*) many."

If these lists are examined carefully then two interesting facts become evident. In the first place there is the prominence of *hyper* in group (3). In that group every text has this preposition except Mark 10:45, and the more Grecized versions of Mark 10:45 in 1 Tim. 2:6 and Titus 2:14 both have it. Then, in the second place, it is very obvious that groups (2) and (3) are quite distinct from one another. Here, at least three points can be noted: (a) In group (2) every text except Rom. 4:25 is apologetic in intent, stressing the divine and scriptural necessity for the passion. Rom. 4:25, on the other hand, with its "for our trespasses" calls attention to the soteriological significance of the passion. In group (3) every text is soteriological in intent; uniformly they echo Rom. 4:25 in stressing the soteriological significance of the passion. (b) In group (2) the dominant title is Son of Man which is found in every text except Rom. 4:25, which is distinctive theologically, and 1 Cor. 11:23. In group (3), however, Son of Man is to be seen only in Mark 10:45 and in a possible influence in 1 Tim. 2:6 (man). (c) Thirdly, as the original division shows, the two groups use (*para*)*didonai* differently.

In view of these facts it is not too much to say that we have evidence of the existence of the two distinct traditions using (*para*)*didonai* of the passion in the New Testament: (1) an apologetic (*para*)*didonai* tradition using the verb in the passive with Son of Man as the characteristic title; and (2) a soteriological (*para*)*didonai* tradition using the verb in the active with a reflexive object and, apart from Mark 10:45, with titles other than Son of Man.

A major feature of the discussion of these texts has been the question of the influence of Isaiah 53 upon them. Which of them alludes to Isaiah 53? Here there is a measure of agreement between Jeremias, Tödt, and Hahn, and also some disagreement. The matter may be summed up as follows:

(a) Rom. 8:32 alludes to the LXX of Isaiah 53.[2]

(b) Mark 10:45 alludes to Isaiah 53 and the allusion was originally in a Semitic language.[3]

(c) Rom. 4:25 alludes to Isaiah 53 and the allusion was originally in a Semitic language.[4]

(d) There is disagreement about the texts using *(para)didonai* in the active with a reflexive object and the preposition *hyper*, i.e., our group (3). Jeremias[5] claimed that there is a *hyper*-formula which is itself an allusion to Isaiah 53 whereas Tödt[6] would recognize such an allusion only in texts which include "a phrase similar to one in Isaiah 53" and Hahn[7] in these texts and also in those using the characteristic "many" or "all." On this point the evidence does seem to indicate that *hyper* alone is insufficient to indicate an allusion to Isaiah 53. It is agreed by Jeremias, Tödt, and Hahn that Mark 10:45, "a ransom for many" (using *anti*) alludes to Isaiah 53. When this text is Grecized in 1 Tim. 2:6, this becomes "a ransom for all" (using *hyper*) and when it is further developed in Titus 2:14 it is simply "for us" (using *hyper*). If the first two of these texts allude to Isaiah 53, then so does the third.

A point we have to recognize in this connection is that the allusions in these traditions are not always directly to Isaiah 53, but rather to a tradition within the church of using Isaiah 53 to

---

2. Jeremias, *Servant of God*[2], p. 89 n. 399d; Tödt, *Son of Man*, p. 160; Hahn, *Titles*, p. 60.

3. Jeremias, *Servant of God*[2], p. 90 n. 401; Tödt, *Son of Man*, 203; Hahn, *Titles*, p. 57.

4. Jeremias, *Servant of God*[2], p. 89 n. 397; Tödt, *Son of Man*, p. 160; Hahn, *Titles*, p. 60.

5. Jeremias, *Servant of God*[2], pp. 89, 95–96.

6. Tödt, *Son of Man*, p. 161.

7. Hahn, *Titles*, p. 56.

interpret the cross of Christ. This tradition begins in a Semitic language (Mark 10:45; Rom. 4:25), but is most highly developed in Greek. When the tradition moves into Greek it adopts the characteristic preposition *hyper*, which is not in the LXX of Isaiah 53 where the prepositions are *dia* and *peri*,[8] and *hyper* then becomes a key word in this tradition. Its dominance can be seen not only from its strength in the sequence Mark 10:45, 1 Tim. 2:6, Titus 2:14, but also from the fact that it is found in all the texts in our group (3)—except for Mark 10:45—and from the further fact that it is dominant in the actual use of the preposition in statements about the death of Christ in the New Testament. According to Jeremias's count *hyper* is found 37 times to *peri* 8 times, *dia* 3 times, and *anti* once.[9]

The question of the origin (or origins) of these uses of (*para*)-*didonai* in connection with the passion in the New Testament must now be raised and it is here that this paper has a particular hypothesis to offer. This hypothesis may be summarized as follows:

(a) (*Para*)*didonai* developed as a technical term to be used of the passion of Jesus. At this stage the word was descriptive and it had no particular theological connotation.

(b) In early Christian passion apologetic a number of Old Testament passages were used in connection with the passion. This apologetic practice interacted with the use of (*para*)*didonai* to produce the apologetic (*para*)*didonai* tradition. Isaiah 53 was not one of these traditional apologetic texts.

(c) Isaiah 53 came to be used of the passion in developing a soteriology of the cross rather than an apologetic for it. This must first have happened in a Semitic language sphere and the earliest phase of this known to us is preserved by Rom. 4:25. Then this soteriological use of Isaiah 53 has interacted with a Son of Man saying to produce Mark 10:45, still in a Semitic language. But the major development here takes place in Greek. In the Hellenistic church the inherited practice of using Isaiah 53 soteriologically is developed in connection with the use of (*para*)*didonai* to give us

8. Jeremias, *Servant of God*[2], p. 95.
9. Ibid., pp. 95–96.

the soteriological *(para)didonai* tradition. Now something must be said about each one of these stages.

(a) **The use of** *(para)didonai* **as a technical term for the passion:** That the early Christians did use the verb as a technical term in connection with the passion is uniformly acknowledged: the verb occurs frequently in the passion narrative itself; Judas is formally designated "the betrayer"; and in 1 Cor. 11:23 "on the night when he was betrayed" clearly means "on the night when the passion began."

What is the origin of this use of *(para)didonai*? Hahn makes the interesting suggestion that "to deliver into someone's hands" might have become an established phrase in Jewish literature dealing with the fate of prophets[10] and the Christians may have adopted it from such a source. This is entirely possible as it is clear that it is a terminology appropriate to the fate of any godly man. In Mark 1:14 and Matt. 4:12 it is used of John the Baptist. The point that must be made is that in this use the verb is purely descriptive. For all that it is an extremely emotive word, and for all that it may carry with it overtones of the fate of prophets and men of God, the verb *(para)didonai* does not of itself have any particular theological significance. As it stands in the New Testament texts it is neither apologetic nor soteriological in tendency; it is simply wholly appropriate and vividly descriptive. For this reason it is very doubtful if the origin of this use of the verb lies in Isaiah 53, despite the fact that *(para)didonai* itself occurs three times in the LXX version of that chapter (verse 6 and twice in verse 12).

In the New Testament this descriptive use of *(para)didonai* is certainly the earliest that is found in connection with the passion of Jesus. Perhaps because of a usage in Jewish literature in connection with the fate of prophets, certainly because it is a word of great emotional force, the verb is used by Christians in connection with the passion of Jesus. Moreover, this use is Semitic and not Greek[11] which indicates that it has its beginning in early Palestinian Christianity.

10. Hahn, *Titles*, p. 39 n. 150.
11. Tödt, *Son of Man*, p. 160 (*Menschensohn*, p. 148) following Schlatter.

(b) The development of an apologetic *(para)didonai* tradition: The use of *(para)didonai* in connection with the passion first becomes theological as the verb is used in early Christian passion apologetic. This use develops either with reference to specific Old Testament texts, especially Psalm 22 and Psalm 118, or by the use of a word or phrase deliberately alluding to the apologetic use of such texts. The first of the Markan passion predictions, Mark 8:31, has both of these traits. *Dei* must be seen as a reference to the divine necessity for the passion revealed in scripture, and "be rejected" *(apodokimasthēnai)* is a reference to Ps. 118 (LXX 117):22, a verse extensively used by early Christians in this connection. Mark 8:31 is therefore emphatically apologetic in tone, and since the whole section Mark 8:27–10:52 has been very carefully composed by the evangelist,[12] this same emphasis must be held to be dominant also in Mark 9:31 and 10:33–34, the more so since neither of these texts develop any soteriological emphasis at all. A further text in this section of Mark, Mark 9:12, has been held to introduce a note from Isaiah 53, and hence what I would call a soteriological overtone, in its "be treated with contempt" *(exoudenēthë)*. Both Jeremias[13] and Lindars[14] hold this to be an allusion to Isa. 53:3, where in some Greek versions (but not in LXX) we find *exoudenōmenos*. Against this, however, three considerations must be urged. (1) Both the specific reference to scriptural fulfillment and the general tone of the saying are in harmony with the passion prediction, creating the impression of apologetic rather than soteriology. (2) The *exoudenēthē* is explicable as a reference to Ps. 22 (LXX 21): vs. 7 *exoudenēma*; vs. 25 *exoudenōsen*, a Psalm which the passion narrative itself shows was extensively used in early Christian passion apologetic. (3) Acts 4:11: "the stone which was rejected" *(exouthenetheis)* can be held to reflect a combination of allusions to Psalms 118 and

---

12. Tödt, *Son of Man,* pp. 145–147. The evidence for Markan compositional activity and for a careful threefold repetitive pattern in Mark 8:27–10:52 is very striking. I have called attention to it in detail in an article, "The Literary *Gattung* 'Gospel': Some Observations," *Expository Times.*
13. Jeremias, *Servant of God*[2], p. 90 n. 406.
14. Barnabas Lindars, *New Testament Apologetic* (1961), p. 81.

22. Such freedom with regard to the text of the Old Testament would be by no means uncommon in Qumran or early Christian *pesharim*.

Mark 14:41 also has this characteristic apologetic overtone for it clearly parallels and echoes 14:21: "... the Son of Man goes as it is written of him," which has the explicit reference to the fulfillment of scripture.

We have then a series of texts, all alluding to scripture, but not to Isaiah 53—all developing passion apologetic and all using *(para)didonai*: we have an apologetic *(para)didonai* tradition.

It should be further noted that in this apologetic *(para)didonai* tradition the tendency is to use the verb in the passive. This is the passive which expresses the divine activity and its use is an indication of the Semitic overtones of this tradition and of its age. It certainly goes back to earliest Palestinian Christianity.

(c) **The development of a soteriological *(para)didonai* tradition:** If the thesis of this paper is correct, that the texts in using *(para)didonai* in the passive, group (2), are apologetic in intent and do not refer to Isaiah 53—except for Rom. 4:25—then that throws the use of Isaiah 53 into sharp perspective. It means that Isaiah 53 is used (i) in Rom. 4:25; (ii) in Mark 10:45; 1 Tim. 2:6; Titus 2:14; (iii) in Gal. 1:4; 2:20; Eph. 5:2; 5:25; (iv) in Rom. 8:32. This is exactly the order in which we should consider them.

(i) Rom. 4:25: This is generally accepted as pre-Pauline and it certainly alludes to Isaiah 53, corresponding to the Targum of Isa. 53:5b.[15] Two other things about the text should be noted: it has the passive of *paradidonai* and it uses *dia* rather than the *hyper* which established itself so strongly in the Hellenistic Christian traditions. All these are indications of the comparative age of the saying; it can certainly be argued that this is the earliest use of Isaiah 53 in connection with the passion that we have in Greek-speaking Christianity, and that it is a product of an interaction between the traditional use of *paradidonai* (especially in the passive) to refer to the passion and the use of Isaiah 53 to interpret the cross, both of which go back to Palestinian Christianity.

15. Jeremias, *Servant of God*², p. 89 n. 397.

(ii) **Mark 10:45:** This is uniformly seen by Jeremias, Tödt, and Hahn as an allusion to Isaiah 53, and as an allusion to that chapter in a Semitic language. I can only agree and point out again that here we have a text which antedates the use of *hyper* in this connection, as that *hyper* forces out the *anti* in 1 Tim. 2:6 and Titus 1:4.

In regard to the origin of Mark 10:45 I advance the following hypothesis, a hypothesis which both accounts for the data and arises out of points made in the recent discussion:

(a) It was originally an I-saying about service of the type now represented in an independently developed Hellenistic form by Luke 22:27.

(b) The I-saying about service was transformed into a Son of Man saying reflecting upon the significance of the ministry of Jesus as the ministry of the Son of Man. There was a very definite tendency in early Christianity to reflect on the significance of the ministry of Jesus as the ministry of the Son of Man as can be seen from Matt. 13:37: "He who sows the good seed is the Son of Man," and Luke 19:10: "The Son of Man came to seek and to save the lost." "The Son of Man came not to be ministered to but to minister" would fit into such a category of sayings very readily but, at the same time, it would cry out for a subsequent gloss.

(c) The Son of Man saying about the significance of the ministry of Jesus as the ministry of the Son of Man is then glossed from the tradition to use Isaiah 53 of the passion and our Mark 10:45 is produced and ultimately translated into Greek.

A particular feature of Mark 10:45 to which I would call attention is the fact that "to give his life" makes the Son of Man a much more active figure than the Lord of Rom. 4:25, who is "put to death (*paredothē*) for our trepasses," i.e., he is the passive object of another's handling, or than the Son of Man of the apologetic (*para*)*didonai* tradition, who is the passive object of God's handling. This makes Mark 10:45 younger than the apologetic (*para*)-*didonai* tradition, and it also indicates that Rom. 4:25 reaches back to a theological stage earlier than that represented by Mark 10:45.

(iii) Gal. 1:4; 2:20; Eph. 5:2; 5:25: These texts represent the third stage in the use of Isaiah 53. That text is now being used in Greek and in particular it is represented by the *hyper* which characterizes Hellenistic Christian references to it. Moreover, we have, as in Mark 10:45, the central figure actively "giving himself" although since the tradition has now become thoroughly Greek, that figure is no longer designated Son of Man. This is the soteriological (*para*)*didonai* tradition in all its fullness.

(iv) Rom. 8:32: This text need not detain us for a moment. It is an independent allusion to the LXX of Isa. 53:6 and testifies to the use of that text by Paul rather than to any particular tradition in the church. Professor Hahn suggested to me in private conversation that it may well have roots in a traditional way of speaking of God's "sending" his Son and that it represents a comparatively late stage of Pauline theological reflection, successive to Gal. 4:4–5 and Rom. 8:3–4. I find this highly probable. Certainly Rom. 8:32 is the final development of the soteriological use of (*para*)*didonai* in connection with the passion of Jesus and theologically speaking the youngest of the texts that have concerned us.

POSTSCRIPT

The reader will have noticed that in this article I use the form *(para)didonai* whereas earlier I had used only *paradidonai*. The reason is that when I came to examine the traditions in detail I realized that one could not distinguish between *paradidonai* as, for example, in the passion predictions, and *didonai*, as, for example, in Mark 10:45. The parallelism of meaning between Gal. 1:4, which uses *dontos*, and Gal. 2:20, using *paradontos*, shows that the two forms of the verb are synonymous, as indeed we would expect in *koine* Greek. However it is interesting to note that *didonai* is found only in the soteriological tradition, which I claim is the latest of the traditions to develop. This would seem to indicate that the traditions began with a technical use of *paradidonia* but that as they developed the synonym *didonai* also came to be used.

CHAPTER VIII

The Christology of Mark:
A Study in Methodology

Contemporary scholarly investigation of the Synoptic Gospels is dominated by redaction criticism (*Redaktionsgeschichte*),[1] the key to which is the ability to distinguish material used by the evangelist and the literary activity of the evangelist in editing, to determine the theology of the evangelist. The conviction is that one can do this by observing his literary activity in redaction and composition. In the cases of Matthew and Luke[2] this has worked well, because we have a firm basis to work on as we observe their use of Mark and of the sayings source Q.[3] In the past several years we have had real breakthroughs in our understanding of the theology of these two evangelists, and redaction critics have established a firm basis for work in this area.[4] But in the case of the Gospel of

1. Joachim Rohde, *Rediscovering the Teaching of the Evangelists* (1969; see also my *What is Redaction Criticism?* (1969).
2. I am using the names Matthew, Luke, and Mark to designate both the Gospel and evangelist concerned, adding further definition only where necessary to avoid confusion or for emphasis. This usage is for convenience only and is not intended to make any statement about the traditional authorship of the Gospels.
3. Redaction critics uniformly accept the two-source hypothesis of the Synoptic Gospels and regard the successful results of their work as an added substantiation of it.
4. Both Rhode and I review this work in the books mentioned in note 1 above. Unfortunately there is as yet no full-scale presentation in English of the theology of Matthew and Luke as we now understand it in the light of the work of the redaction critics. Tragically, Hans Conzelmann,

Mark we have had no such basis for our work, and as yet we have had no such breakthrough in connection with the theology of the second evangelist (Mark).

The problem in connection with Mark is one of method. Redaction criticism in this case is possible only to a limited extent, and it needs to be supplemented by other critical methods. As yet there is no scholarly consensus with regard to what particular blend of methods should be used in an historical investigation of the Gospel of Mark and the theology of the second evangelist. It is the purpose of this paper to suggest such a blend and then to attempt to demonstrate the possibility inherent in the particular approach suggested by carrying out a sample investigation of an aspect of the theology of the evangelist, namely, his Christology.

One aspect of our approach to the Gospel of Mark must be that of redaction criticism itself. Despite the difficulties inherent in the fact that we have none of Mark's sources, we must make a serious attempt to separate tradition from redaction and to determine the literary activity of the evangelist. The main thrust of contemporary work on Mark is along these lines, and there are several ways of attempting to isolate Markan redaction. One is to use the literary factors of vocabulary and style. Examples of this approach would include the work of Eduard Schweizer and his pupil, Ulrich Luz,[5] or of Ehrich Grässer or Johannes Schreiber.[6] Another way is to pay careful attention to particular Markan concerns, such as the messianic secret, the geographical location Galilee (which in Mark has a more-than-geographical reference) or the use of Son of Man. A recent example of this approach is Etienne Trocmé's *La formation de l'évangile selon Marc* (1963), with its chapters "Les an-

---

the leading redaction critic to work on Luke and the author of the breakthrough in connection with his Gospel, has treated the matter most inadequately in his recently published *Outline of the Theology of the New Testament* (1969).

5. Eduard Schweizer, "Anmerkungen zur Theologie des Markus," in *Neotestamentica* (1963), pp. 93–104; and Ulrich Luz, "Das Geheimnismotiv und die Markinische Christologie," *ZNW* 56 (1965), pp. 9–30.

6. Erich Grässer, "Jesus in Nazareth," *NTS* 16 (1969/70), pp. 1–23; Johannes Schreiber, "Die Christologie des Markusevangeliums," *ZTK* 58 (1961), pp. 261–268, and *Die Theologie des Vertrauens* (1967).

tipathies manifestées par l'évangeliste" and "Les causes défendues par Marc." A third way is to pay careful attention to Markan compositional techniques: the use of intercalation, the fondness for threefold units, the practice of using related stories as parentheses to enclose a major unit, and so on. Ernst Lohmeyer in Germany and R. H. Lightfoot in England pioneered in this approach during the 1930s, and it still remains a feature of the work of English scholars.[7] A fourth way is to attempt to isolate definite units of pre-Markan tradition and then to observe Mark's use of these units. L. E. Keck did this with a cycle of miracle stories and its introduction,[8] and I attempted it with the Son of Man Christology.[9] In these and still other ways scholars attempt to identify Markan redaction of tradition and to proceed along the currently well-established lines of *Redaktionsgeschichte*. But a major fact about Mark's Gospel is that it is a new creation—there was nothing like it before in early Christian literary history—and this leads to a second line of approach to the Gospel: the search for a model.

Prior to the writing of Mark there was no extended narrative gospel. There were connected units of tradition—a passion narrative, cycles of miracle stories, collections of sayings, collections of parables, an apocalyptic discourse, perhaps short collections of stories with a geographical center such as Capernaum or the Sea of Galilee, and so on—but no connected narrative beginning with John the Baptist and ending with the passion and/or resurrection (depending upon one's views of the current ending of the Gospel at 16:8). So Mark was creating a new literary genre, and the question is: "What does the literary form he creates tell us about his purpose in writing?" Or, to put it another way, "What literary

7. Ernst Lohmeyer, *Das Evangelium des Markus* (1937); R. H. Lightfoot, *History and Interpretation in the Gospels* (1934); idem, *Locality and Doctrine in the Gospels* (1938); idem, *The Gospel Message of St. Mark* (1950; paperback, 1962). Two recent works by English scholars embodying this approach are: T. A. Burkill, *Mysterious Revelation* (1963); and D. E. Nineham, *Saint Mark* (1963).

8. Leander E. Keck, "Mark 3:7–12 and Mark's Christology," *JBL* 84 (1965), pp. 341–358.

9. See my essay "The Creative Use of the Son of Man Traditions by Mark," *USQR* 23 (1967/68), reprinted above as Chapter VI.

model is he following?" In the days when the Gospel of Mark was regarded as fundamentally a life of Jesus or a chronicle of the ministry of Jesus, this question did not arise, but with the widespread acceptance of the fact that the Gospel is neither a life nor a chronicle it does arise, and today it is being strenuously debated. The most widely accepted view is that Mark's Gospel is "a passion narrative with an extended introduction" (Martin Kähler), and many contemporary interpretations of the Gospel proceed from this premise. This view does justice to Mark's theology of the cross, but it seems not to do justice to his eschatology. Another view being pressed at the moment is that Mark's Gospel is fundamentally an aretalogy, having grown out of a cycle of stories presenting Jesus as a divine man.[10] In conscious opposition to this latter view, Howard Kee is arguing that Mark is to be understood in apocalyptic terms,[11] a view which I would support. This debate is only just getting underway, but it clearly is important. Our interpretation of Mark will depend very much upon any decision we make as to the model he is following—as to his purpose in writing as this is revealed in the literary form he is creating or imitating.

A consideration of the literary form of the Gospel of Mark leads to a third aspect of our approach to the work: an approach via the insights of general literary criticism. The Gospel of Mark is after all a literary text, and it should therefore be interpreted according to the canons of literary criticism. We should observe such things as the movement of the "plot," the roles of the protagonists— especially perhaps Peter and the disciples—the literary structure of the total work, and so on. The evangelist Mark may not be an author in the conscious and sophisticated sense of a William Shakespeare, Henry Fielding, or James Joyce, but he is an author, he has written a literary work, and he must be treated from the standpoint of literary criticism.

10. Morton Smith, "Aretalogies, Divine Men, the Gospels, and Jesus," (paper presented to the Society for Biblical Literature Seminar on the Gospels, New York, Autumn 1970); cf. Moses Hadas and Morton Smith, *Heroes and Gods: Spiritual Biographies in Antiquity* (1965).

11. Howard C. Kee, "Aretalogy and the Gospels" (paper prepared in response to Morton Smith's at the SBL Seminar on the Gospels); cf. Kee, *Jesus in History* (1970), pp. 104–147.

It is my contention that each of these three avenues of approach to the evangelist Mark and his Gospel must be explored, and that the three approaches must be held in tension with one another. No one of them is the key to the whole, but together they offer us the opportunity to come close to Mark and his theology as redaction criticism has brought us to Matthew and Luke and their theologies.[12] As a *Probe*, I turn to the question of the Christology of Mark.

A consideration of the Christology of Mark can begin with a literary point: the importance to the Gospel of 14:53–71, the trial before the Sanhedrin and the denial by Peter. Here many of the themes which play a major role in the Gospel as a whole reach a climax. In verse 62, the messianic secret is unveiled, and in Peter's denial both the theme of the disciples' "hardness of heart" and Peter's role as leader of the disciples reach a tragic climax which Aristotle would have recognized. From a literary standpoint these scenes are climactic of what has gone before and preparatory of what is to come after—the account of the crucifixion.

We can reenforce the importance of these scenes to Mark by observing the amount of Markan literary activity in them. The trial scene (verses 55–65) is intercalated between references to Peter in the *aulē* (verses 54, 66), a Markan composition and technique and itself bears strong evidence of Markan vocabulary and style.[13]

From the standpoint of Christology, the trial scene offers an important point. In verse 61, Jesus is addressed as Christ and Son of God; in verse 62 he accepts these designations and immediately

12. It goes without saying that considerations of model/purpose and of literary criticism will be helpful in the case of Matthew and Luke also. But their model is Mark, so even here their redaction of Mark will be the indispensable key.

13. John Donahue, S.J., a student of mine working on the trial narrative, presented to the Catholic Biblical Association meeting in the summer of 1970 the following evidence of Markan literary activity in the narrative: (1) the use of the impersonal third person plural in introductory sentences with Jesus as the object of a verb in the same context; *kai* parataxis compound of *erchomai*; the historic present; use of *pas* or *holos* to *universalize* a scene (twenty instances of this in Mark): (2) sentence with the order *kai*-participle-subject; tautologous repetition of key words or phrases as in verses 56, 59 (forty-seven instances of this in Mark) as "a Markan insertion technique" (Donahue's own discovery); and more. See now his *Are You the Christ? The Trial Narrative in the Gospel of Mark* (1973).

interprets them by means of a use of Son of Man: "Are you the Christ, the Son of the Blessed?" (61). And Jesus said, "I am; and you will see the Son of Man sitting at the right hand of Power, and coming with the clouds of heaven" (62).[14]

A very similar thing happens at Caesarea Philippi. Now the Caesarea Philippi pericope (Mark 8:27–9:1) is also very important from the standpoint of a literary critical approach to the Gospel of Mark. As lives of Jesus without number testify, it is the watershed of Mark's literary composition. Furthermore, it also shows strong evidence of Markan literary activity.[15] At Caesarea Philippi Jesus is confessed as the Christ. He implicitly accepts this confession (not explicitly as in 14:62 because according to Mark's literary device it is not yet time for the messianic secret to be unveiled) and immediately goes on to interpret the designation in terms of a use of Son of Man: "Peter answered him, 'You are the Christ' [29]. And he began to teach them that the Son of Man must suffer" (31). At two key points in his literary composition, therefore, Mark has Jesus interpret and give content to the titles Christ and Son of God by using Son of Man.

Thus far we have approached the Christology of Mark by considering literary points—the role of the trial and denial and of the Caesarea Philippi pericope in the plot of the Gospel as a whole— and reenforcing those by considering the redaction critical point of Markan literary activity in those pericopes. In other words, we have used the third and the first of the approaches advocated at the beginning of this paper. Now we will turn to the second: a consideration of the model Mark might be following and of what this will tell us of his purpose in writing. In this regard we have to admit at once that the discussion has not yet reached the point of a consensus as to the model for the Gospel as a whole, and therefore

14. I quote the RSV but use Son of Man rather than the Son of man of that version from here on.

15. The parallelism between 8:31 ff.; 9:31 ff.; 10:32 ff (passion prediction-misunderstanding-teaching) shows that everything in the pericope after verse 31 is Markan. Moreover the passion prediction itself is Markan composition (as I shall argue later in this paper), and the teaching in verses 8:34–9:1 has been heavily edited and in part actually composed by Mark (Perrin, *What is Redaction Criticism?* pp. 44–51.)

of an agreement as to Mark's overall purpose in writing. But although we have no agreed model for the Gospel as a whole, scholarship does recognize models—and hence purposes—for certain aspects or parts of it. In particular it would be agreed that Mark inherits and uses the model of the synoptic tradition itself. From its earliest days the Palestinian church used the form of sayings of Jesus and stories about him in preaching, in parenesis, in controversy and apologetic. A Son of Man saying exhorting to penitence, wisdom-type teaching to instruct in the essential preparation for the coming, controversies between the early believers and their Jewish brethren in the form of stories about Jesus and Pharisees, apologetic for the cross in the form of Jesus showing its divine necessity from the scriptures, all this and more is Mark's heritage and most immediate model. So we can say with confidence that the Gospel of Mark is in part *didactic narrative*. The form is a narrative of the ministry of Jesus, but the concerns are those of Mark and his church, and the purpose is directly to exhort, instruct, and inform Mark's readers.

Thus far we can go by general agreement, but we can go one step further because there would also be general agreement that a major aspect of the Markan purpose is christological: he is concerned with correcting a false Christology prevalent in his church and to teach both a true Christology and its consequences for Christian discipleship. I have discussed this matter at some length elsewhere,[16] and therefore I may here simply assert the fact that Mark is concerned with correcting a false Christology, the point I argued earlier, and go on to make some further points in more detail.

An analysis of the literary structure of the Gospel reveals the importance of the three passion prediction units (8:31–9:1; 9:30–37; 10:32–45). Each has exactly the same structure (prediction-misunderstanding-teaching), and each is a form of an in-

---

16. *What is Redaction Criticism?* pp. 53–56. T. J. Weeden's work, which was a catalytic agent for me in this matter, has now been summarized in an article, "The Heresy That Necessitated Mark's Gospel," *ZNW* 59 (1968), pp. 145–158, and published as a book, *Mark: Traditions in Conflict* (1971).

terpretation of Peter's confession. The fact that there are three of them is certainly due to Mark's concern for threefold repetition. As has often been noted they are part of basic structure of the section of the Gospel (8:27–10:45) in which Mark presents his *theologia crucis*. In these interpretations of Peter's confession, Mark is presenting his own passion-oriented Christology, using Son of Man, and then drawing out its consequences for Christian discipleship: in the first, the necessary preparedness Jesus exhibited; in the second, the necessity of servanthood; in the third, the climactic presentation of servanthood culminating in the ransom saying. At no point in the Gospel, except for the discourse in chapter 13, is Mark so clearly addressing and exhorting his own readers. The dynamic use of the form of sayings and stories of Jesus in the synoptic tradition has here become a literary convention, a convention which Mark establishes, develops, and adheres to strictly. The disciples set the stage by asking the questions or voicing the tendencies or opinions (and these are the questions, tendencies, and opinions present in Mark's church) and Jesus exhorts and teaches. So far as Christology is concerned, Peter confesses Jesus as the Christ but then exhibits a false understanding of the meaning of that confession, in all of which he is representing Mark's church. The true Christology is then expressed by Jesus using Son of Man, and adhering to the convention, Son of Man is never found in Mark except on the lips of Jesus.[17] There is one

17. This is important in the context of the fact that nowhere in the Gospels is Son of Man found except on the lips of Jesus (for one possible exception see note 24 below); a fact from which it is often argued that Jesus did use the term as a self-designation, and the tradition has remained true to him in this regard. The fact does however admit of an alternative explanation, admittedly more complex. In the first place Son of Man is not a christological title. It is rather a designation for Jesus in his apocalyptic authority, derived from Daniel 7 and then used in the paradox of the necessity for his passion ("the Son of Man goes as it is written of him . . . is betrayed" [Mark 14:21]). It is never used confessionally and it tended not to survive the movement of the church into the Greek-speaking world (in the formula like 1 Thess. 1:10, Jesus is expected from heaven as Son of God, not Son of Man. In the Hellenized version of Mark 10:45 found in 1 Tim. 2:5, it is not the Son of Man but "the man Christ Jesus" who gave himself as a ransom for all). In the synoptic tradition before Mark, all the sayings are in the form of words of Jesus, including the Son of Man sayings. Mark develops the use of Son of Man very extensively, as we shall argue below, but he

possible exception to this, Mark 2:10. The abrupt change of subject and the tautologous repetition of the command to the paralytic indicate that the Son of Man saying may be an aside addressed by the evangelist to his readers (see note 24 below). So a consideration of a possible model for an aspect of Mark's Gospel and of an aspect of his overall purpose leads us to a point already recognized: Mark uses Son of Man to correct and give content to a christological confession of Jesus as the Christ.

We can reach a similar point with regard to Son of God if we concentrate upon the first of our recommended approaches to the Gospel, the separation of redaction from tradition and the careful observation of the use made of tradition. Since Karl Ludwig Schmidt's epoch-making investigation of *Der Rahmen der Geschichte Jesu* (1919), it has been generally recognized that Mark 3:7–12 is a Markan *Sammelbericht* (redactional summary) and hence, more recently, that it, together with other summaries, is of great importance for a redaction critical investigation of Mark.[18] Mark 3:7–12 was further studied by Leander E. Keck[19] who showed that it introduces a cycle of miracle stories in which Jesus is portrayed as a Hellenistic *theios anēr* (3:7–12; 4:35–5:43; 6:31–52; 6:53–56) and that Mark is concerned with playing down and correcting this understanding of Christology, as can be seen both from his redaction of the introduction and from his redaction of the cycle of stories themselves (especially the intro-

---

has the convention of restricting it, the true Christology, to the lips of Jesus. Luke never uses the expression except in dependence upon a source, and the additional uses by Matthew and John are not extensive enough to break the conventions of the synoptic tradition and of Mark, especially in view of the total absence of any confessional use of Son of Man as a christological title. So it is possible to account for the evidence in the Gospels without recourse to the hypothesis that Jesus used the expression as a self-designation in a way more meaningful than in an idiomatic expression such as "the Son of Man came eating and drinking," where it seems to be simply a circumlocution whereby the speaker refers to himself. See my article "The Son of Man in the Synoptic Tradition," *Biblical Research* 13 (1968), reprinted above as Chapter V.

18. A student of mine investigated the summaries from the viewpoint of Mark's Christology: Vernon Robbins, "The Christology of Mark" (University of Chicago Divinity School dissertation, 1969).

19. Keck, note 8 above; cf. Robbins, pp. 77–103, where Keck's insights are taken up and developed further.

duction of the secrecy motif). The outlook of the original tradition
was that of Jesus as a *theios anēr*, and Mark's own understanding
of the Son of God category is sufficiently different from these
stories to enable us to infer that he took them into his Gospel
partly because they allowed him to present the divine sonship
during Jesus' lifetime and partly because he wanted "to check and
counterbalance this way of understanding Jesus' life and work."[20]
Thus, on the basis of a redaction critical investigation, Keck
reached a conclusion similar to that which we have reached on
other grounds.

I am moving toward the point of claiming that the Christology
of Mark may best be approached by assuming that he uses "Christ"
and "Son of God" to establish rapport with his readers and then
deliberately reinterprets and gives conceptual content to these titles
by a use of "Son of Man," a designation which is not, properly
speaking, a christological title but which to all intents and purposes becomes one as Mark uses it. Let me now approach this
matter from the viewpoint of observing the occurrence of these
three titles in Mark, paying attention to their place in the literary
structure of the Gospel and to their relation with one another.

20. Keck, p. 358. More recently Paul Achtemeier has published the
first part of an extended study of the pre-Markan tradition of miracle
stories and its use by the evangelist in his "Towards the Isolation of
pre-Markan Miracle Catenae," *JBL* 89 (1970), pp. 265–291. He argues
for a rather different analysis of the pre-Markan material, seeing two
cycles of stories (catenae), as does Keck, but claiming that they are
symmetrical, with each including a sea miracle, three healings, and a
feeding. Catena I is Mark 4:35–5:43; 6:34–44, 53, and Catena II is
Mark 6:45–51; 8:22–26; 7:24b–30, 33–37; 8:1–10. I find myself in
agreement with many of Achtemeier's observations, but I have three reser-
vations about his division. In the first place such symmetry is itself
suspicious. Then, second, the second group of three healings (the Blind
Man at Bethsaida, the Syrophoenician Woman, and the Deaf Mute,
8.22–26; 7:24b–30; 7:32–37) is not homogenous. The first and third
exhibit a common concern for healing techniques, but the second has
the same aura of healing by fiat that is characteristic of Achtemeier's
Catena I (the Gerasene Demoniac, The Woman with the Hemorrhage,
Jairus's Daughter, 5:1–20; 5:25–34; 5:21–23, 35–43). Last, Keck's argument about the relationship with the subsequent cycle of stories is an important factor. Publication of the remaining parts of Achtemeier's study
may change the situation, but at the moment I am personally inclined
to stay with Keck's analysis and conclusions, except that I would add
the Syrophoenician Woman to his cycle of miracle stories originally presenting Jesus as a *theios anēr* and now being reinterpreted by Mark.

"Christ" is to be found in Mark at 1:1; 8:29; 9:41; 12:35; 13:21; 14:61; 15:32. From the viewpoint of literary structure, three of these seven occurrences are comparatively unimportant: 9:41 with its parenetic use of "you are Christ's"; 13:21, a reference to false Christ is in the apocalyptic discourse;[21] and 15:32, the mocking at the cross. A fourth, 12:35 where Christ is not the Son of David, is more difficult. It may be that Mark is here correcting a Son of David Christology as elsewhere he corrects christologies associated with Christ and Son of God, but I must admit that as yet I have no firm opinion with regard to the function of the Son of David pericope in the Gospel of Mark. But the remaining three are all at key points in the Gospel: 1:1 is the superscription defining the whole work as "the gospel of Jesus Christ"; 8:29 is the confession at Caesarea Philippi; and 14:61 is the High Priest's question at the trial. In 1:1 the title is associated with Son of God in some textual traditions; in 8:29 and 14:61 it is immediately interpreted by a use of Son of Man.

In connection with my contention that Mark is concerned with correcting a false Christology prevalent in the church of his day, one should note how many of these references are to a false use of "Christ"; 8:29 (an immediate correction by a use of Son of Man); 13:21 (the false Christs); 14:61 (an immediate reinterpretation using Son of Man); 15:32 (the mocking). Although Mark clearly intends the title to represent the full and proper Christian confession, especially in the central Caesarea Philippi pericope, in his Gospel there is no correct human christological confession of Jesus until we come to the Centurion in 15:39. The Centurion uses Son of God which is the most important title so far as Mark is concerned as he addresses his readers, as we shall see immediately below. Although it is not the one by means of which he expresses

---

21. Even if this reference should be of real significance for an understanding of the historical occasion for the writing of Mark, it is not a significant reference in terms of the Markan Christology. That the reference is of real significance for the historical understanding of Mark has been strongly argued by a student of mine, Werner H. Kelber in his "Kingdom and Parousia in the Gospel of Mark" (University of Chicago Divinity School dissertation, 1970), pp. 151–159; this work, in revised form is being published in 1974 by Fortress Press as *The Kingdom in Mark: A New Place and a New Time*.

his own Christology. He could not use it for that purpose because it could never have been made to bear the range of meaning he intended to fuse into his own Christology. The correct confession by the Centurion is possible because by 15:39 the literary process of correcting the Christology held by Mark's readers is complete, having been completed by Jesus' response to the High Priest's question at the trial.

"Son of God" (or its equivalent) is to be found in Mark six or seven times, always at places which are important to the Gospel as a whole. According to some textual traditions it is part of the superscriptions in 1:1.[22] Then it occurs at each of the places in the Gospel where cosmic phenomena (heavens opening, or the like) indicate a revelatory moment according to the conventions of the first century C.E.: 1:11, the baptism; 9:7, the transfiguration. Then it occurs twice on the lips of demons, creatures whose supernatural origin would indicate supernatural knowledge in the world in which Mark lived and for which he wrote: 3:11 (in a redactional summary); 5:7. Finally it is linked with "Christ" in the High Priest's question, 14:61, and in 15:39 it is the confession of the Centurion in what is clearly for Mark a climactic moment.

It can be seen that neither "Christ" nor "Son of God" is especially frequent in Mark, but that the former is found at key moments in the narrative and that every occurrence of the latter is significant. "Son of Man" occurs much more frequently than either, a total of fourteen times: 2:10; 2:28; 8:31; 9:9; 9:12; 9:31; 10:33; 10:45; 13:26; 14:21 (twice); 14:41; 14:62. The sheer frequency of occurrence of this title indicates its importance for Mark; but at the same time it presents problems to the interpreter, for the fact is that the usage does not immediately appear to be homogenous. A comparatively crude division is that into three: present authority, 2:10; 2:28; apocalyptic, 8:38; 13:26; 14:62; suffering, 9:12; 10:45; 14:21(twice); 14:41; 8:31; 9:31; 10:33. But that leaves one unaccounted for, 9:9, and the third group is

22. In view of the importance of this title in Mark one is tempted to say that if it was not part of the original superscription it should have been, and the scribe who first added it was Markan in purpose if not in name!

not really a group at all. To say the very least, the predictions, 8:31; 9:31; 10:33; have to be separated from the rest as having an internal cohesiveness of their own. At the same time it is possible to account for each occurrence in terms of inherited tradition, Markan development of that tradition, and creation of new tradition, and by doing this to reach the heart of the Christology of Mark. To this task we now turn.

We will begin with 9:9, the redactional command to secrecy "until the Son of Man be risen from the dead." It would be generally acknowledged that this is Markan redaction and, equally, that it is important to an understanding of the secret and of the Markan purpose altogether. In the Gospel of Mark the transfiguration is proleptic of the parousia,[23] and this saying directs Mark's readers to the post-resurrection pre-parousia situation in which they stand and to which Mark is directing the teaching he puts on the lips of Jesus. That the saying uses Son of Man is due in part to the fact that it is Mark's own designation of Jesus and also probably in part to the proximity of the predictions of the passion and resurrection. In any case, the saying is readily explicable and understandable as a Markan hint to his readers as to his own understanding of his purpose in writing.

Let us take next the two references to the Son of Man's authority on earth in the present of the ministry of Jesus, "the Son of Man has authority on earth to forgive sins" (2:10), and "the Son of Man is Lord even of the sabbath" (2:28). I have argued elsewhere that these represent a particularly Markan development of a tendency at work in the synoptic traditions,[24] and I would repeat

23. A point I expect to argue in some detail in a subsequent publication, a book, *Towards the Interpretation of the Gospel of Mark*, to be published by SCM Press on which I am currently at work.
24. See "The Creative Use of the Son of Man Traditions by Mark," Chapter VI above. The point that 2:10 is Markan can now be strengthened by two further observations. The first of these is the anacoluthon which makes the Son of Man reference read very like a comment by the evangelist addressing his readers, rather as he does in 13:14. Prof. J. A. Fitzmyer suggested to me verbally that this may be one instance where Son of Man is not on the lips of Jesus in the Gospel. The second is that the tautological repetition of the command to the paralytic may indicate that we have here an example of the Markan insertion technique identified by John Donahue (note 13 above).

that here. Only in Mark and in dependence on Mark is *exousia* used of the earthly ministry of Jesus in the Synoptic Gospels, and from a literary standpoint these two references to the Son of Man stand dramatically in the section of the Gospel in which the authority of Jesus in word and deed is being thematically presented (1:16–3:6). There are no further references to the Son of Man until it begins to play its dominant role in the central interpretative section of the Gospel (8:27–10:45). The movement toward the view of Jesus' earthly ministry as already exhibiting his full authority is to be found in the synoptic tradition, for example, Matt. 8:9 par., but it is Mark who first takes the step of using *exousia* of that earthly ministry and linking it with Son of Man. Moreover, there is real literary artistry in the two uses of Son of Man in the first major section of the Gospel which are followed by two uses of Son of God in the second (3:11 and 5:7 in the section 3:7–6:6a). The two are thereby established as equivalent designations for Jesus in his full authority, and the way is prepared for the interpretation of the latter in terms of the former which is a fundamental part of Mark's christological concern. The use of Son of Man in 2:10 and 2:28 therefore fits smoothly into Mark's overall concern.

The three uses of Son of Man in apocalyptic context in Mark, 8:38; 13:26; 14:62, present no problems. I have discussed them all at some length elsewhere,[25] and may simply reiterate the conclusion that 8:38 is a Markan redaction of a *Satz heiligen Rechtes* (Käsemann) just as that now found in Luke 12:8–9 par., 13:26 is an early Christian apocalyptic promise, and 14:62 a product of early Christian midrash-pesher use of the O.T.[26] What we have here is the use by Mark of early Christian tradition: 8:38 juxtaposes with 8:31 in the Caesarea Philippi pericope, and so provides the basis for the full development of Mark's Son of Man Christol-

25. See my *Rediscovering the Teaching of Jesus* (1967), pp. 185–191, 173–185.

26. This last conclusion received strong support in Matthew Black's presidential address to the Studiorum Novi Testamenti Societas in August, 1970, where he demonstrated the strong evidence that now exists for such a use of the Old Testament by early Christians in the development of Kyrios, Son of God, and Son of Man Christologies. The address has been published *NTS* 18 (1971/72), pp. 1–14.

teaching on discipleship in the passion prediction units and in this way to link that teaching decisively to the Son of Man Christology which for him is its essential basis.

(3) In 14:21, 41 we have an apologetic use of Son of Man with the verb *paradidonai* whereby the passion of Jesus is summarized by the verb, which means to betray, deliver up, and the stress is on the divine necessity for the passion. The link between Son of Man and the verb (*para*)*didonai* in connection with the passion is pre-Markan,[31] and in that sense Mark 14:21, 41 are traditional, whatever the actual history of the Gethsemane material may be in the synoptic tradition and in Mark's Gospel. As they stand, these Son of Man sayings are Markan echoes of traditional early Christian passion apologetic. All passion narratives in the New Testament are saturated with such notes, including Mark's.

(4) The real problem with regard to Markan composition is presented by the predictions of the passion and resurrection, 8:31; 9:31; 10:33–34. The three most recent discussions of this matter, all from an avowedly redaction critical standpoint, show a steady progression toward recognition of Markan literary activity: H. E. Tödt thought all three were traditional; Ferdinand Hahn that the first and second were, the third being Markan; and George Strecker that the first was, the second and third being Markan.[32] It is my personal conviction that all three have been composed by Mark, who has mined their constituent parts from the (*para*)-*didonai* tradition and the passion apologetic of earliest Christianity.[33] Be that as it may, the use of the predictions by Mark is not in dispute. He uses them to develop the passion-oriented element of his own Christology and to form the basis for the consequent

---

31. For the justification of this and subsequent statements about the use of (*para*)*didonai* in the tradition, see the article mentioned in note 30 above.

32. Tödt, *Son of Man*, pp. 152–221; F. Hahn, *The Titles of Jesus in Christology* (1969), pp. 37–42; G. Strecker, "The Passion and Resurrection Predictions in Mark's Gospel," *Interpretation* 22 (1968), pp. 421–442.

33. This, too, will be argued in the subsequent publication referred to in note 23 above, on the basis that (1) the verbal parallelism of the last part of the predictions indicates a common origin; (2) there is no known *Sitz im Leben* for them as units apart from their *Sitz im Evangelium des Markus*; and (3) that there is evidence for the prior existence of their separate parts in the tradition of the church.

teaching on the essential nature of discipleship which follows each of them in the stereotyped pattern of the three passion-prediction units (8:36–9:1; 9:30–37; 10:32–45).

The position with regard to the Son of Man Christology in the tradition prior to Mark and the Markan use of that tradition now becomes clear. Prior to Mark there are three uses of Son of Man in the tradition: use in an apocalyptic context, use in reflection upon the significance of the ministry of Jesus, probably in a Eucharistic setting, and use with (*para*)*didonai* in apologetic for the passion. From these beginnings Mark develops the threefold emphasis which is characteristic of his Gospel—apocalyptic, authority in the present, suffering—and all the references to Son of Man in the Gospel become explicable on the basis of this hypothesis of inherited tradition and Markan development of it. Beyond this, an approach to the Gospel along the three avenues of redaction criticism, the question of model or purpose, and general literary criticism shows that Mark is using Son of Man to express his own Christology; that he uses Christ and Son of God to establish rapport with his readers, and Son of Man to interpret and give content to those titles. It is not the claim of this paper that these conclusions are new—on the contrary they would generally be accepted by the world of scholarship—but it is the claim of the paper that the fact that they can be reached by the approach suggested validates that approach and suggests a similar approach to other aspects of the Markan theology and purpose.

CHAPTER IX

Reflections
from a Way Station

It can be seen that what began for me as a concern for rediscovering the teaching of Jesus has become a concern for method in the interpretation of the Gospel of Mark, and that for the time being my pilgrimage in New Testament Christology is at an end. My current concern for the passion predictions and for Mark 10:45 is in the context of the theology of Mark rather than in that of the Christology of the New Testament, although it will be obvious by now that for me the theology of Mark is a very important aspect of the Christology of the New Testament. But I am conscious of being, so to speak, at a way station. The work of one decade is now ended and that of another is beginning. I suspect that in the next decade I shall have occasion to return to Life of Jesus research, as well as to the Christology of the New Testament in general and the Son of Man in the New Testament in particular, but these will no longer be the main foci of my academic concern. However, before leaving in 1973 the work that began in 1961 I may perhaps be permitted to offer some general reflections upon it.

THE USE OF SON OF MAN IN THE GOSPEL OF JOHN

First, I would like to reflect upon something which I have not done, which is to investigate the use of Son of Man in the Gospel of John. I am very conscious of the fact that competence in the world of Johannine studies demands specialized knowledge and techniques which I simply do not possess but, at the same time, a decade of concentration upon the Son of Man in the synoptic tradition and the Gospel of Mark does give me a standpoint from which I may offer some observations upon the Son of Man in the Gospel of John.

The Son of Man occurs in the Gospel of John as follows:

1:51: "You will see heaven opened, and the angels of God ascending and descending upon the Son of Man."

3.13: "No one has ascended into heaven but he who descended from heaven, the Son of Man."

6:62: "Then what if you were to see the Son of Man ascending where he was before?"

3:14: "As Moses lifted up the serpent in the wilderness, so must the Son of Man be *lifted up*."

12:34: "The crowd answered him, 'We have heard from the law that the Christ remains forever. How can you say that the Son of Man must be *lifted up*? Who is this Son of Man?' "

8.28: "So Jesus said, "When you have *lifted up* the Son of Man, then you will know that I am he, and that I do nothing on my own authority but speak thus as the Father taught me. . . .' "

5:27: "[The Father has given the Son] authority to execute judgment, because he is the Son of Man."

6:27: "[Labor for] the food which endures to eternal life, which the Son of Man will give to you; for on him has God the Father set his seal."

6:53: "Unless you eat the flesh of the Son of Man and drink his blood, you have no life in you." Verse 54: ". . . my flesh . . . my blood."

9:35: "Do you believe in the Son of Man?"

12:23: "The hour has come for the Son of Man to be glorified."

13:31: "Now is the Son of Man glorified, and in him God is glorified."

In addition to these there are a number of references to Son of God which must also be considered:

1:34: [John witnesses] "I have seen and hence born witness that this is the Son of God."

1:49: "Nathanael answered him, 'Rabbi, you are the Son of God! You are the King of Israel.' "

3:18: "He who believes in him is not condemned; he who does not believe is condemned already, because he has not believed in the name of the only Son of God."

5:19–24: Dialogue on the relationship between the Father and the Son.

5:25: ". . . the dead will hear the voice of the Son of God, and those who hear will live."

10:36: " 'I am the Son of God.' "

11:4: "This illness . . . is for the glory of God, so that the Son of God may be glorified by means of it."

11:27: "I believe that you are the Christ, the Son of God, he who is coming into the world."

20:31: ". . . these are written that you may believe that Jesus is the Christ, the Son of God."

17:1: "Father, the hour has come; glorify thy Son that the Son may glorify thee."

19:7: "The Jews answered him, 'We have a law, and by that law he ought to die, because he made himself the Son of God.' "

Now, of course, to a specialist in the Synoptic Gospel material an obvious thing about these texts is their difference from anything he has been investigating heretofore. Almost the only thing that would be familiar is the shift from the Son of Man to the first person pronoun in 6:53–54 for this occurs, for example, in Matt. 10:32 = Luke 9:26. But the kind of uses with which he is familiar, the Son of Man "coming on the clouds of heaven," the Son of Man who "must suffer many things," and so on, these are all conspicuous by their absence. Perhaps the nearest thing to the synoptic use is John 5:27, for to say that the Son has "authority (*exousia*) to execute judgment because he is the Son of man" is obviously another way of saying that "the Son of Man has authority (*exousia*) on earth to forgive sins" (Mark 2:10). One should note the use of *exousia* which in this context in the synoptic materials is found only in Mark and in dependence on Mark. But there seems to be a slight but perhaps significant difference even between these two sayings, namely, that the Johannine is more reflective in tone. Whereas the Markan saying proclaims the authority of Jesus as Son of Man the Johannine saying reflects upon that authority, but then that is a fundamental difference in style between the two evangelists. John reflects and Mark proclaims.

But much the most obvious thing about the Johannine Son of Man sayings to anyone who reads them as a group is that they express a distinctive Christology. They cohere to present Jesus as the redeemer who descended from heaven to bring life to the believer and who then ascended again to the Father, having achieved that for which he was sent. One could not wish for a more distinct presentation of Christ as the descending-ascending heavenly redeemer than that to be found in the Johannine Son of Man sayings. Now, however, if one looks elsewhere in the New Testament for other expressions of this particular Christology then one does not find it in the synoptic Son of Man sayings but in the great christological hymns which form criticism has detected at various places, e.g., Phil. 2:6–11; 1 Tim. 3:16; 1 Pet. 3:18–22.[1]

Phil. 2:6–11:
> "Who, being in the form of God,
>> Did not think it robbery to be equal with God,
>> But emptied himself.
>> Taking the form of a slave.
>> Becoming in the likeness of men
>> And being found in fashion like a man
>> He humbled himself,
>> Becoming obedient unto death.
>> Wherefore God highly exalted him
>> And bestowed on him the name above every name
>> That in the name of Jesus every knee may bow in
>>> the heavens and on earth,
>> And every tongue confess,
>> 'Jesus Christ is Lord!' "

1 Tim. 3:16:
> "Who was mainfested in the flesh,
>> was vindicated in the spirit,
>> was seen by angels,
>> was proclaimed among the nations,
>> was believed on in the world,
>> was taken up in glory."

1. I am here following Jack T. Sanders, *New Testament Christological Hymns* (1971).

1 Pet. 3:18–22:

> "Having been put to death in the flesh,
> Having been made alive in the spirit,
> Having gone to the spirits in prison,
> He preached.
> Who is at the right hand of God,
> Having gone into heaven,
> Angels and authorities and powers having
> been made subject to him."

The Johannine Son of Man sayings are nearer to these hymns in their Christology than they are to the synoptic Son of Man sayings and their Christology.

The Johannine Son of Man sayings, I would therefore claim, express a distinctive Christology—the Christology of Christ as the descending-ascending heavenly redeemer—which is a Johannine development of the Christology to be found in the christological hymns. The contours of this Christology would seem to owe more to the world of Hellenism, perhaps mediated through the Hellenistic Jewish wisdom movement, than to the world of Jewish and Christian apocalyptic. But more important than the question of its ultimate origins is the fact that this is a Christology which is characteristic of the Gospel of John in general; it is expressed elsewhere in the Gospel than in the Son of Man sayings. Let us look, for example, at the prologue, John 1:1–11:

> In the beginning was the Word,
> And the Word was with God,
> And the Word was God.
> He was in the beginning with God.
> Everything was made through him,
> And apart from him was nothing made which was made.
> In him was life.
> And the life was the light of men.
> And the light shines in the darkness
> And the darkness did not overcome it.
> He was the true light,
> Which enlightens every man,
> Coming into the world.
> He was in the world,

And the world was made through him.
And the world did not know him.
He came to his own.
And his own did not receive him.

The contours of the Christology being expressed here are clearly the same as those of the Christology being expressed in the Son of Man sayings.

Further, these same christological contours are to be found in the Gospel of John in connection with the title Son (of God). In John 3:17: "God sent the Son into the world"; in 5:25: "the dead will hear the voice of the Son of God, and those who hear will live"; in 10:31: the Son of God is he "who the Father consecrated and sent into the world"; and in 17:1, 5: Jesus prays, "Father, the hour has come; glorify thy Son that the Son may glorify thee . . . glorify thou me in thy own presence with the glory which I had with thee before the world was made." All this is very close to the kind of thing we find in the Son of Man sayings. The titles may vary, but the Christology is constant and that Christology is the Christology of the Gospel of John. Indeed the titles Son of God and Son of Man are virtually interchangeable as is evident from 5:25–27: ". . . the hour is coming, and now is, when the dead will hear the voice of the Son of God, and those who hear will live . . . [for the Father] has granted the Son also to have life in himself, and has given him authority to execute judgment, because he is the Son of Man." What we find in the Gospel of John is a constant Johannine Christology which comes to varied expression in the Prologue and by the use of Son of Man and Son of God in the Gospel.

At the same time, however, the Johannine Son of Man sayings do echo some of the notes found in the synoptic Son of Man sayings, especially those found in the Gospel of Mark. Let us compare Mark 14:62 and John 1:51.

Mark 14:62	John 1:51
"I am;	"you will see
and you will see	heaven opened,
the Son of Man	and the angels of

sitting at the right	God ascending
hand of Power,	and descending
and coming with the	upon the Son of Man"
clouds of heaven."	

If we recognize the fact that the Gospel of John has a characteristic lack of interest in the Son of Man "coming with the clouds of heaven," and such recognition would seem to be unavoidable, then John 1:51 looks extraordinarily like a Johannine redaction of Mark 14:62, or to put it another way, like a translation of Mark 14:62 into a Johannine idiom.

The second point of contact between the Markan and Johannine use of Son of Man we have already noted, that between Mark 2:10 and John 5:27.

Mark 2:10	John 5:27
"But that you may	"[The Father has given the
know that	Son]
the Son of Man	*exousia*
has *exousia* on earth	to execute judgment,
to forgive sins."	because he is the Son of Man."

In an earlier essay I argued that this use of *exousia* is characteristically Markan and its use in John 5:27 in a Son of Man saying does seem to me to indicate Johannine knowledge of the Gospel of Mark, rather than of general synoptic Son of Man traditions, particularly when taken in conjunction with John 1:51 and its relationship to Mark 14:62, for Mark 14:62 is, in my view, distinctively Markan rather than traditional.

To summarize these reflections on the Son of Man in the Gospel of John, then, we may say that Son of Man in John is used to express a distinctively Johannine Christology, a Christology which is also expressed in other ways in the Gospel. At the same time the use of Son of Man in John does exhibit some points of contact with earlier uses of Son of Man in the New Testament and its traditions, particularly the use of Son of Man by the evangelist Mark.

THE USE OF SON OF MAN BY THE EVANGELIST MARK

It will be obvious to the reader of these essays that my understanding of the Markan use of Son of Man has gradually developed
and indeed is still developing. On this point my opinions have
changed almost from publication to publication and I can only
hope that these changes will be seen as, in Victor Furnish's words,
part of "a true pilgrimage" and not of an "aimless peregrination."
The problem for me has been that of my particular academic heritage. I first approached the Gospel of Mark in the context of Life
of Jesus research and was therefore constantly and solely absorbed
in the question of whether or in what form the Son of Man sayings
in Mark went back to Jesus. When I broke in turn out of that
mold I did so under the impact of form criticism and of redaction
criticism in its narrower form of the observation of the redaction
of existing tradition. This latter was a particular challenge in the
case of the Gospel of Mark because for Mark we had no such
access to the sources the evangelist had used as we had in the cases
of the Gospels of Matthew and Luke. But we could, I believed
(and still do believe), reconstruct the pre-Markan use of Son of
Man and then observe Mark's redaction and use of this traditional
Son of Man material. This I set out to do and the results of that
endeavor are evident in the essays reprinted above. Rereading
those essays today I am myself surprised to see how long it took
me to recognize the true extent of "the creative use of the Son of
Man by Mark." Inhibited by my concern for Markan redaction of
tradition I first recognized the extent of Mark's literary activity in
connection with the Son of Man sayings in the central section of
the Gospel, 8:27–10:45, and then in the careful juxtaposition of
Son of Man and Son of God in the earlier part of the Gospel. But it
has literally taken me years to get beyond that and my treatment
of the occurrences of Son of Man after 10:45 fully deserves the
trenchant criticism of Hendrikus Boers:

> Perrin's correct insight that the importance of the Son of Man
> sayings for Mark is an important clue for our understanding

of the Gospel does not appear to have led to an equally successful investigation of these sayings in the Gospel.[2]

The logic of the results of my own work should long ago have brought me to recognize that the evangelist is every bit as active in the composition and use of Son of Man sayings after 10:45 as he is between 8:27 and 10:45 and before 8:27.

The Son of Man sayings in Mark after 10:45 are as follows:

13:26: "And then they will see the Son of Man coming in clouds with great power and glory."

14:21: "For the Son of Man goes as it is written of him, but woe to that man by whom the Son of Man is betrayed (*paradidotai*)!"

14:41: ". . . the Son of Man is betrayed (*paradidotai*) into the hands of sinners."

14:62: "I am; and you will see the Son of Man sitting at the right hand of power, and coming with the clouds of heaven."

The apocalyptic saying in 13:26 has recently been reinvestigated by John Donahue as part of an investigation of the "future" Son of Man sayings as a group in the Gospel of Mark.[3] He shows that "the details which characterize the coming of the Son of Man—in glory, on the clouds of heaven, with power, accompanied by angels—are peculiar to the future Son of Man sayings as they are found in Mark and in the traditions dependent upon him."[4] This is a most important discovery because it means that we have to reckon with a very considerable element of Markan redaction in both 13:26 and also in 8:38. In both cases we probably have to envisage at least a traditional future Son of Man saying which Mark has reworked, and it may be that we have to go further and envisage sayings which Mark himself has created out of constituent traditional elements. This latter is the conclusion toward which I now incline, not least because I have reached a similar conclu-

2. Hendrikus Boers, "Where Christology Is Real. A Survey of Recent Research on New Testament Christology," *Interpretation* 26 (1972), pp. 300–327, especially 315.

3. John R. Donahue, *Are You the Christ? The Trial Narrative in the Gospel of Mark* (1973).

4. Ibid., p. 154.

sion about Mark 9:1 which with 8:29 forms the climax to the Caesarea Philippi pericope.[5] But in any case Donahue's work makes it clear that both 13:26 and 8:29 exhibit signs of considerable Markan redaction.

The situation with regard to 13:26 is further complicated by the whole question of the apocalyptic discourse in the Gospel of Mark. This has become a focal point of scholarly discussion today, particularly since Lars Hartman showed how much the discourse has in common with similar discourses in Jewish apocalyptic, and since Willi Marxsen, Theodore Weeden, and Werner Kelber showed how much the discourse reflects Mark's own situation, interests, and concerns.[6] It is not yet clear how these two divergent tendencies in current research into Mark 13 can be reconciled. My own working hypothesis is that 13:1–5a form an introduction to the discourse, giving it a setting in the Gospel and composed by the evangelist: 13:5b–27 are the discourse proper, and 13:28–37 are a parenthetical conclusion composed by the evangelist. Within the discourse itself we have to reckon with considerable Markan redaction, especially in verses 9 and 26 and perhaps at other places also. I am aware that to say "perhaps at other places also" is to beg the really important questions about the whole chapter but I could only approach those questions in the context of a discussion of the Gospel as a whole.

Mark 14:21 and 41 reflect the use of *paradidonai* in the "apologetic *paradidonai* tradition" I investigated in my essay for the Jeremias *Festschrift*, reprinted above. They therefore at least contain traditional elements but, again, a more detailed discussion would necessarily involve a discussion of the Gethsemane pericope as a whole and its function in the Gospel. But Boers is probably right about 14:41:

> Mark 14:41 evidently performs a crucial function in the transition which combines Christ's resolute intention to go up to

---

5. See my *What is Redaction Criticism?* 145–151.
6. Lars Hartman, *Prophecy Interpreted*; Willi Marxsen, *Mark the Evangelist*, pp. 151–206; Theodore J. Weeden, *Mark—Traditions in Conflict*, passim; Werner Kelber, *The Kingdom in Mark: A New Place and a New Time*.

Jerusalem to die (8:27–14:41) with his passiveness in the actual passion narrative.[7]

In that case we have to reckon with considerable Markan literary activity in 14:41. An immediately attractive hypothesis would be, then, to see tradition in 14:21 and redaction, or even Markan composition, in 14:41. But the matter clearly demands further intensive investigation.

With regard to Mark 14:62, Donahue has investigated this saying further in the context of an investigation of the trial narrative as a whole[8] and shown that it does indeed serve the crucial purpose of providing the climactic statement of Mark's own Christology and the final reinterpretation of Son of God by means of a use of Son of Man. I am growing increasingly skeptical of the possibility that it ever existed as a saying prior to the writing of the Gospel of Mark and increasingly inclined to view it as a literary production of the evangelist himself, a conclusion Donahue argues with regard to the whole trial narrative. Mark may well be mining Christian traditions in the saying but he himself created it in its present form and gave it its present setting in the Gospel to serve his own purpose in writing.

All in all it can be seen that I am now no longer of the opinion that 13:26; 14:21; 14:41; and 14:62 are "traditional sayings allowed to stand in material taken over by Mark." My present view would be that 14:21 may be traditional but 13:26 shows considerable Markan redaction while 14:41 and 14:62 are literary creations of the evangelist himself, although he may well be mining Christian tradition for their constituent parts.

In these last few paragraphs I have clearly moved from the Christology of the New Testament to the interpretation of the Gospel of Mark and at this point I may therefore be permitted to turn from the concern of one decade of my academic pilgrimage to that of another.

7. Boers, "Where Christology Is Real," pp. 316–317.
8. Donahue, *Are You the Christ?*, pp. 172–181.

Bibliography

The main purpose of this bibliography is to give publication details of works mentioned in the text of the book. In addition to this an attempt has been made to give a reasonably comprehensive bibliography of the discussion of "Son of Man" since the publication of H. E. Tödt, *The Son of Man in the Synoptic Tradition* (See below).

Achtemeier, Paul. "Towards the Isolation of a pre-Markan Miracle Catenae." *Journal of Biblical Literature* 89 (1970): 265–291.

Ashby, E. "The Coming of the Son of Man." *Expository Times* 72 (1960): 360–363.

Baeck, Leo. *Judaism and Christianity*. New York: Atheneum, 1970.

Barrett, C. K. "Stephen and the Son of Man." *Apophoreta: Festschrift für Ernst Haenchen*. Beihefte zur *ZNW* 30, pp. 32–38. Berlin: Alfred Töpelmann, 1964.

Betz, Hans Dieter, ed. *Christology and a Modern Pilgrimage: A Discussion with Norman Perrin*. Claremont, California: The New Testament Colloquium, 1971.

Birdsall, J. N. "Who is this Son of Man?" *Evangelical Quarterly* 42 (1970): 7–17.

Black, Matthew. *An Aramaic Approach to the Gospels and Acts*. 3d ed. Oxford: Clarendon Press, 1967.

———. "The Christological Use of the Old Testament in the New Testament." *New Testament Studies* 18 (1971/72): 1–14.

———. "Eschatology of the Similitudes of Enoch." *Journal of Theological Studies* n.s. 4 (1953): 1–10.

———. "The 'Son of Man' Passion Sayings in the Gospel Tradition." *Zeitschrift für die neutestamentliche Wissenschaft* 60 (1969): 1–8.

———. "The Son of Man Problem in Recent Research and Debate." *Bulletin of the John Rylands Library* 45 (1962/63): 305–318.

Boers, Hendrikus. "Psalm 16 and the Historical Origin of the Christian Faith," *Zeitschrift für die neutestamentliche Wissenschaft* 60 (1969): 106–110.

————. "Where Christology Is Real: A Survey of Recent Research on New Testament Christology," *Interpretation* 26 (1972): 300–327.

Bornkamm, Günther. *Jesus of Nazareth.* New York: Harper & Row, 1960. German original, 1956.

Bornkamm, Günther; Barth, G.; and Held, H. J. *Tradition and Interpretation in Matthew.* Philadelphia: Westminster Press, 1963. German original, 1960.

Borsch, Frederick H. *The Christian and the Gnostic Son of Man.* Studies in Biblical Theology, 2d series, vol. 14. London: S.C.M. Press, 1970.

————. "The Son of Man," *Anglican Theological Review* 45 (1963): 174–190.

————. *The Son of Man in Myth and History.* London: S.C.M. Press, 1967.

Bousset, Wilhelm. *Die Religion des Judentums im späthellinistischen Zeitalter.* Edited by H. Gressmann. 3d ed. Tügingen: J. C. B. Mohr (P. Siebeck), 1926.

————. *Kyrios Christos.* Nashville: Abingdon Press, 1970. German original, 1913.

Bultmann, Rudolf. *The History of the Synoptic Tradition.* Oxford: Basil Blackwell, 1963, rev. ed. 1968. German original, 1st ed. 1921, 5th. ed. 1961.

Burkill, T. A. "The Hidden Son of Man in St. Mark's Gospel," *Zeitschrift für die neutestamentliche Wissenschaft* 52 (1961): 189–213. Reprinted in his *New Light on the Earliest Gospel.* Ithaca, N.Y.: Cornell University Press, 1972.

————. *Mysterious Revelation.* Ithaca, N.Y.: Cornell University Press, 1963.

Cambe, M. "Le fils de l'homme dans les évangiles synoptiques," *Lumière et Vie* 12 (1963): 32–64.

Charles, R. H. (ed.) *Apocrypha and Pseudepigrapha of the Old Testament.* 2 vols. Oxford: Clarendon Press, 1913.

Colpe, Carsten. "ho huios tou anthrōpou." *Theologisches Wörterbuch zum Neuen Testament* VIII (1969): 403–481.

Coppens, J. "Le Fils de l'homme daniélique et les relectures des Dan. 7:13 dans les Apocryphes et les éscrits du Nouveau Testament." In Coppens, J. and Dequeker, L., *Le Fils d'homme et les saints du Très-Haut en Dan. 7 dans les Apocrophes et dans le Nouveau Testament.* Bruges: 1961.

Cortes, J. B. and Gratti, F. M. "The Son of Man or Son of Adam." *Biblica* 49 (1968): 467–502.

Cullmann, Oscar. *The Christology of the New Testament.* Philadelphia: Westminster Press, 1959. German original, 1957.

Dibelius, Martin. *From Tradition to Gospel.* New York: Charles Scribner's Sons, 1935. German original, 1919; 4th ed. 1961.

Donahue, John. *Are You the Christ? The Trial Narrative in the Gospel of Mark.* Society of Biblical Literature Dissertation Series, vol. 10, 1973.

Duling, Dennis C. "Tradition of the Promises to David and His Sons in Early Judaism and Primitive Christianity." Ph.D. dissertation, University of Chicago Divinity School, 1970.

Edwards, Richard A. *The Sign of Jonah in the Theology of the Synoptic Gospels and Q.* Studies in Biblical Theology, 2d series, vol. 19. London: SCM Press, 1972.

Emerton, J. A. "The Origin of the Son of Man Imagery." *Journal of Theological Studies* n.s. 9 (1958): 225–242.

Enslin, Morton Scott. *The Prophet from Nazareth.* New York: McGraw-Hill, 1961.

Foakes-Jackson, F. J. and Lake, Kirsopp, eds. *The Beginnings of Christianity.* 5 vols. New York: Macmillan, 1920–33.

Ford, J. M. "The Son of Man—Euphemism?" *Journal of Biblical Literature* 87 (1968): 257–266.

Formesyn, R. E. C. "Was There a Pronominal Connection for the *Bar Nasha* Self-Designation?" *Novum Testamentum* 8 (1966): 1–35.

Freed, E. D. "The Son of Man in the Fourth Gospel." *Journal of Biblical Literature* 86 (1967): 402–409.

Fridrichsen, Anton. "Le péché contre le Saint-Esprit." *Revue d'Histoire et de Philosophie Religieuses* 3 (1923): 367–372.

Fuller, Reginald H. *The Foundations of New Testament Christology.* New York: Charles Scribner's Sons, 1965.

Gaston, L. *No Stone on Another.* Leiden: E. J. Brill, 1970.

Gelston, A. "A Sidelight on the Son of Man." *Scottish Journal of Theology* 22 (1969): 189–196.

Glasson, T. F. "The Ensign of the Son of Man, Matt. 24:30." *Journal of Theological Studies* n.s. 15 (1964): 299–300.

Goppelt, Leonhard. "Zum Problem des Menschensohnes—Das Verhältnis von Leidens—und Parusieankündigung." *Mensch und Menschensohn. Festschrift für K. Witte.* Ed. H. Sierig. Hamburg: F. Wittig, 1963.

Grässer, Erich. "Jesus in Nazareth." *New Testament Studies* 16 (1969/70): 1–23.

Hadas, Moses and Smith. Morton. *Heroes and Gods: Spiritual Bi-*

ographies in Antiquity. Freeport, N.Y.: Books for Libraries Press, 1965.

Hahn, Ferdinand. *The Titles of Jesus in Christology.* New York: The World Publishing Co., 1969. German original, 1963, 2d. ed. 1964.

Hamerton-Kelly, R. G. *Pre-Existence, Wisdom and the Son of Man.* S.N.T.S. Monograph Series, no. 21. New York: Cambridge University Press, 1973.

Hartman, Lars. *Prophecy Interpreted. The Formation of Some Jewish Apocalyptic Texts and of the Eschatological Discourse Mark 13 par.* Lund: C. W. K. Gleerup, 1966.

Haufe, G. "Das Menschensohn-Problem in der gegenwärtigen wissenschaftlichen Diskussion." *Evangelische Theologie* 26 (1966): 130–141.

―――. "Le problème du fils de l'homme." *Études Théologiques et Religieuses* 424 (1967): 311–322.

Higgins, A. J. B. "Is the Son of Man Problem Insoluble?" *Neotestmantica et Semitica: Studies in Honour of Matthew Black.* Ed. E. E. Ellis and M. Wilcox. Edinburgh: Clark, 1969.

―――. *Jesus and the Son of Man.* Philadelphia: Fortress Press, 1964.

―――. *Menschensohn-Studien.* Franz Delitzsch–Vorlesungen, 1961. Stuttgart: Kohlhammer Verlag, 1965.

―――. "The Sign of the Son of Man (Matt. 24:30)." *New Testament Studies* 9 (1963): 380–82.

―――. "The Son of Man Concept and the Historical Jesus." *Studia Evangelica*, vol. 5, pp. 14–20. Ed. F. L. Cross. Texte und Untersuchungen zur Geschichte der altchristlichen Literatur, vol. 103. Berlin: Akademie Verlag, 1968.

―――. "Son of Man–*Forschung* since the 'Teaching of Jesus.'" *New Testament Essays: Studies in Memory of T. W. Manson.* Ed. A. J. B. Higgins. Manchester: Manchester University Press, 1959.

Hindley, J. C. "Jesus as 'Son of Man' in the Light of Some Recent Discussions." *Bulletin of the Society for Biblical Studies*, 1. Bangalore, India, 1966.

―――. "The Son of Man: A Recent Analysis." *Indian Journal of Theology* 15 (1966): 172–178.

Hodgson, Peter C. "The Son of Man and the Problem of Historical Knowledge." *Journal of Religion* 41 (1961): 91–108.

Hooker, M. D. *The Son of Man in Mark.* London: S.P.C.K., 1967.

Jeremias, Joachim. *Abba. Studien zur neutestamentlichen Theologie und Zeitgeschichte.* Göttingen: Vandenhoeck & Ruprecht, 1966.

―――. "Die älteste Schicht der Menschensohn-Logien." *Zeitschrift für die neutestamentliche Wissenschaft* 58 (1967): 159–172.

————. *The Central Message of the New Testament.* New York: Charles Scribner's Sons, 1965.

————. *New Testament Theology:* Vol. 1, *The Proclamation of Jesus.* New York: Charles Scribner's Sons, 1971.

————. *The Parables of Jesus.* Rev. ed. New York: Charles Scribner's Sons, 1963.

————. See also under Zimmerli, Walther.

Jüngel, Eberhard. *Paulus und Jesus: Untersuchungen zur Präzisierung der Frage nach dem Ursprung der Christologie.* Tübingen: J. C. B. Mohr (Paul Siebeck), 1964.

Käsemann, Ernst. "Sentences of Holy Law in the New Testament." In Käsemann, Ernst, *New Testament Questions of Today,* pp. 66–81. Philadelphia: Fortress Press, 1969.

Keck, Leander E. "Mark 3:7–12 and Mark's Christology." *Journal of Biblical Literature* 84 (1965): 341–358.

Kee, Howard Clark. *Jesus in History: An Approach to the Study of the Gospels.* New York: Harcourt, Brace & World, 1970.

Kelber, Werner H. *The Kingdom in Mark: A New Place and a New Time.* Philadelphia: Fortress Press, 1974.

Kramer, W. *Christ, Lord, Son of God.* Studies in Biblical Theology 50. London: S.C.M. Press, 1966. German original, 1963.

Kuhn, K. G. "Jesus in Gethsemane." *Evangelische Theologie* 12 (1952/53): 260–285.

Leivestadt, Ragnar. "Der apokalyptische Menschensohn—Ein theologisches Phantom." *Annual of the Swedish Theological Institute* 6 (1968): 49–105.

————. "Exit the Son of Man." *New Testament Studies* 18 (1971/72): 243–267.

Lightfoot, R. H. *The Gospel Message of St. Mark.* London: Oxford University Press, 1962.

————. *History and Interpretation in the Gospels.* New York: Harper & Bros. 1934.

————. *Locality and Doctrine in the Gospels.* New York: Harper & Bros., 1938.

Lindars, Barnabas. *New Testament Apologetic.* Philadelphia: Westminster Press, 1961.

Lindeskog, Gösta. "Das Rätsel des Menschensohnes." *Studia Theologica* 22 (1968): 149–174.

Lohmeyer, Ernst. *Das Evangelium des Markus.* ("Meyer" Kommentar) Göttingen: Vandenhoeck & Ruprecht, 1937.

Lohse, Eduard. *Märtyrer und Gottesknecht.* Göttingen: Vandenhoeck & Ruprecht, 1955.

Longnecker, R. N. "Son of Man as a Self-Designation of Jesus." *Journal of the Evangelical Theological Society* 12 (1969): 151–158.

Luz, Ulrich. "Das Geheimnismotiv und die markinische Christologie." *Zeitschrift für die neutestamentliche Wissenschaft* 56 (1965): 9–30.

McKown, C. C. "Jesus, Son of Man: A Survey of Recent Discussion." *Journal of Religion* 28 (1948): 1–12.

Maddox, R. J. "The Function of the Son of Man according to the Synoptic Gospels." *New Testament Studies* 15 (1968): 45–74.

Manson, T. W. *The Teaching of Jesus.* Cambridge: Cambridge University Press, 1963.

Marlow, R. "The Son of Man in Recent Journal Literature." *Catholic Biblical Quarterly* 28 (1966): 20–30.

Marshall, I. Howard. "The Divine Sonship of Jesus." *Interpretation* 21 (1967): 87–103.

———. "The Son of Man in Contemporary Debate." *Evangelical Quarterly* 42 (1970): 66–87.

———. "The Synoptic Son of Man Sayings in Recent Discussion." *New Testament Studies* 12 (1965/66): 327–351.

Marxsen, Willi. *The Beginnings of Christology.* Facet Books, Biblical Series 22. Philadelphia: Fortress Press, 1969. German original, 1960.

Michaelis, W. "John 1:51, Gen. 28:12 und das Menschensohn Problem," *Theologische Literatur-Zeitschrift* 85 (1960): 561–578.

Moe, Olof. "Der Menschensohn und der Urmensch," *Studia Theologica* 14 (1960): 119–129.

Morgenstern, J. "The 'Son of Man' of Dan. 7:13 f.—A New Interpretation." *Journal of Biblical Studies* 80 (1961): 65–77.

Muilenberg, James. "The Son of Man in Daniel and the Ethiopic Apocalypse of Enoch." *Journal of Biblical Studies* 79 (1960): 197–209.

Newman, B. H. "Towards a Translation of the 'Son of Man' in the Gospels." *Bible Translator* 21 (1970): 141–147.

Nineham, D. E. *The Gospel of St. Mark.* The Pelican New Testament Commentaries. Baltimore: Penguin Books, 1963.

Owen, H. P. "Stephen's Vision in Acts 7:55–56." *New Testament Studies* 1 (1954/55): 224–226.

Peake, A. S. "The Messiah and the Son of Man." *Bulletin of the John Rylands Library* 8 (1942): 3–32.

Perrin, Norman. *The Kingdom of God in the Teaching of Jesus.* London: SCM Press, 1963.

————. "The Literary *Gattung* 'Gospel': Some Observations." *Expository Times* 82 (1970): 4–7.

————. *Rediscovering the Teaching of Jesus.* New York: Harper & Row, 1967.

————. *What is Redaction Criticism?* Philadelphia: Fortress Press, 1969.

————. "Wisdom and Apocalyptic in the Message of Jesus." *Proceedings of the One Hundred Eighth Annual Meeting of the Society of Biblical Literature* (ed. Lane C. McGaughy), vol. 2 (1972): 544–570.

————. "The 'Wredestrasse' becomes the 'Hauptstrasse.' " *Journal of Religion* 46 (1966): 296–300.

Proudman, C. L. J. "Remarks on 'The Son of Man.' " *Canadian Journal of Theology* 12 (1966): 128–131.

Quispel, Gillis. "Nathanael und der Menschensohn." *Zeitschrift für die neutestamentliche Wissenschaft* 47 (1956): 281–283.

Ricoeur, Paul. *The Symbolism of Evil.* New York: Harper & Row, 1967.

Robbins, Vernon K. "The Christology of Mark." Ph.D. dissertation, University of Chicago Divinity School, 1969.

Robinson, J. A. T. *Jesus and His Coming. The Emergence of a Doctrine.* London: SCM Press, 1957.

————. *Twelve New Testament Studies.* Studies in Biblical Theology, no. 34. London: SCM Press, 1962.

Rohde, Joachim. *Rediscovering the Teaching of the Evangelists.* Philadelphia: Westminster Press, 1969. German original, 1966.

Rost, L. "Zur Deutung des Menschensohnes in Daniel 7." *Gott und die Götter. Festgabe für E. Fascher.* Ed. G. Delling. Berlin: Evangelische Verlagsanstalt, 1958.

Sanders, Jack T. *New Testament Christological Hymns.* S.N.T.S. *Monograph Series*, no. 15. New York: Cambridge University Press, 1971.

Sandmel, Samuel. "Son of Man in Mark." In Sandmel, S. *Two Living Traditions: Essays on Religion and the Bible*, pp. 166–177. Detroit: Wayne State University, 1972.

Schippers, R. "The Son of Man in Matt. 12:32/Luke 12:10 Compared with Mark 3:28." *Studia Evangelica*, vol. IV, pp. 231–235. Edited by F. L. Cross. Texte und Untersuchungen zur Geschichte der altchristlichen Literatur, vol. 102. Berlin: Akademie Verlag, 1967.

Schmidt, Karl Ludwig. *Der Rahmen der Geschichte Jesu.* Berlin: Trowitzsch & Sohn, 1919.

Schnackenburg, Rudolf. "Der Menschensohn im Johannes-Evangelium." *New Testament Studies* 11 (1964/65): 123–137.

Schreiber, Johannes. "Die Christologie des Markusevangeliums." *Zeitschrift für Theologie und Kirche* 58 (1961): 154–183, 261–268.

―――. *Theologie des Vertrauens.* Hamburg: Furche Verlag, 1967.

Schultz, S. "Maranatha und Kyrios Jesus." *Zietschrift für die neutestamentliche Wissenschaft* 53 (1962): 125–144.

―――. *Untersuchungen zur Menschensohn Christologie im Johannes-Evangelium.* Göttingen: Vandenhoeck & Ruprecht, 1957.

Schweizer, Eduard "Der Menschensohn (zur eschatologischen Erwartung Jesu)." *Zeitschrift für die neutestamentliche Wissenschaft* 50 (1959): 185–209.

―――. *Neotestamentica.* Zurich: Zwingli Verlag, 1963.

―――. "The Son of Man." *Journal of Biblical Literature* 79 (1960): 119–129.

―――. "The Son of Man Again." *New Testament Studies* 9(1962/63): 256–261.

Scott, R. B. Y. "Behold, He Cometh with Clouds." *New Testament Studies* 5 (1955/56): 127–132.

Sidebottom, E. H. "The Ascent and the Descent of the Son of Man in the Gospel of John." *Anglican Theological Review* 39 (1957): 115–122.

―――. "The Son of Man in the Fourth Gospel." *Expository Times* 68 (1956–57): 231–235, 280–283.

Sjöberg, E. K. T. *Der verborgene Menschensohn in den Evengelien.* Lund: C. W. K. Gleerup, 1955.

Smalley, S. S. "The Johannine Son of Man Sayings." *New Testament Studies* 15 (1969): 278–301.

Strecker, Georg. "The Passion–and Resurrection Predictions in Mark's Gospel," *Interpretation* 22 (1968): 421–442. German original, 1967.

Teeple, Howard. "The Origin of the Son of Man Christology." *Journal of Biblical Literature* 84 (1965): 213–250.

Thompson, G. H. P. "The Son of Man: The Evidence of the Dead Sea Scrolls." *Expository Times* 72 (1960/61): 125.

―――. "The Son of Man—Some Further Considerations." *Journal of Theological Studies* n.s. 12 (1961): 203–210.

Tödt, H. E. *The Son of Man in the Synoptic Tradition.* London: SCM Press, 1965. German original, 1959.

Tremel, Y. B. "Le problème de fils de l'homme selon S. Jean." *Lumière et Vie* 12 (1963): 65–92.

Trocmé, Etienne. *La Formation de l'évangile selon Marc*. Paris: Presses Universitaires de France, 1963.

Tyson, J. B. "The Blindness of the Disciples in Mark." *Journal of Biblical Literature* 80 (1961): 261–268.

Vermés, Geza. "The Use of *Bar Nash/Bar Nasha* in Jewish Aramaic." Appendix to Black, Matthew, *An Aramaic Approach to the Gospels and Acts*. 3d. ed. Oxford: Clarendon Press, 1967.

Vielhauer, Philip. *Aufsätze zum Neuen Testament*. Munich: Chr. Kaiser Verlag, 1965. This volume of collected essays includes: "Gottesreich und Menschensohn in der Verkündigung Jesu" (*Festschrift für Günther Dehn* [1957]: 51–79); "Jesus und der Menschensohn. Zur Diskussion mit H. E. Tödt und E. Schweizer" (*Zeitschrift für Theologie und Kirche* 60 [1963]: 133–177); "Ein Weg der neutestamentliche Christologie? Prüfung der Thesen Ferdinand Hahns" (*Evangelische Theologie* 25 [1965]: 24–72); "Erwägungen zur Christologie des Markusevangeliums" (*Zeit und Geschichte. Dankesgabe an Rudolf Bultmann* [1964]: 155–169).

Walker, William O. "The Origin of the Son of Man Concept as Applied to Jesus." *Journal of Biblical Literature* 91 (1972): 482–490.

Weeden, Theodore J. "The Heresy That Necessitated Mark's Gospel." *Zeitschrift für die neutestamentliche Wissenschaft* 59 (1968): 145–158.

———. *Mark—Traditions in Conflict*. Philadelphia: Fortress Press, 1971.

Weinacht, H. *Die Menschwerdung des Sohnes Gottes im Markusevangelium*. Hermeneutische Untersuchungen zur Theologie 13. Tübingen: J. C. B. Mohr (P. Siebeck), 1972.

Wheelwright, Philip E. *Metaphor and Reality*. Bloomington: Indiana University Press, 1962.

Zimmerli, Walther and Jeremias, Joachim. *The Servant of God*. Studies in Biblical Theology 20. London: SCM Press, 1957, rev. ed. 1965.

Indexes

INDEX OF NAMES

Achtemeier, P., 113 n

Baeck, L., 40 n
Barth, G., 2
Black, M., 19, 23, 28, 70, 117 n
Boers, H., 19–21, 129–130, 131–132
Bornkamm, G., 2
Borsch, F. H., 36–37, 119
Bousset, W., 43, 45, 47
Bultmann, R., 41, 53, 54
Burkill, T. A., 106

Colpe, C., 23–24, 26, 27 n, 36 n
Conzelmann, H., 104 n
Cullmann, O., 41

Dibelius, M., 80, 88 n
Dodd, C. H., 12 n
Donahue, J. R., 108 n, 130, 132
Duling, D. C., 7
Duncan, G. S., 12 n

Edwards, R. A., 7, 36 n, 64–65

Foakes Jackson, F. J., 47, 67 n
Fridrichsen, A., 44
Fuller, R. H., 23, 46, 48, 49, 50, 52, 54–55, 57 n, 60, 72 n, 76 n
Furnish, V., 129

Glasson, T. F., 12 n
Grässer, E., 105 n

Hadas, M., 107 n

Hahn, F., 2, 4, 8, 23, 24 n, 57, 75, 77, 94, 97, 99 n, 120
Hartman, L., 5, 131
Held, H. J., 2
Higgins, A. J. B., 23, 57 n, 72 n

Jeremias, J., 8, 42, 52, 65 n, 94, 97, 98, 99, 100
Jüngel, E., 23, 24 n

Kähler, M., 107
Käsemann, E., 62–63, 89
Keck, L. E., 106, 112, 113
Kee, H. C., 107
Kelber, W. H., 114 n, 131
Kramer, W. H., 58
Kuhn, K. G., 77, 86 n

Lake, K., 47, 67 n
Lightfoot, R. H., 106
Lindars, B., 4, 10, 13, 14 n, 16, 19, 75, 76 n, 77, 86 n, 100
Lohmeyer, E., 106
Lohse, E., 118 n
Luz, U., 84 n, 105 n

Manson, T. W., 1, 2, 4, 12 n, 54, 72 n
Marshall, I. H., 55 n
Marxsen, W., 131
Morgenstern, J., 27 n

Nineham, D. E., 106

Peake, A. S., 49, 50

143

Ricoeur, P., 37–39
Robbins, V., 67, 112 n
Robinson, J. A. T., 12 n, 16, 46 n
Rohde, J., 104 n
Rost, L., 27 n

Sanders, J. T., 125 n
Schlatter, A., 99 n
Schmeichel, M., 40 n
Schmidt, K. L., 112
Schreiber, J., 78 n, 84 n, 105 n
Schultz, S., 58
Schweizer, E., 23, 57 n, 67–68, 105 n
Scott, R. B. Y., 12 n
Sjöberg, E., 57
Smith, M., 107
Strecker, G., 90, 120

Taylor, V., 12 n
Teeple, H., 23 n
Tödt, H. E., 2, 3, 4, 6, 8, 22, 23, 24, 43–44, 45, 54, 57 n, 60, 63, 68, 69–70, 73, 75, 77, 80, 86, 89 n, 90 n, 94, 97, 120
Trocmé, E., 105–106
Tyson, J. B., 78 n, 84 n

Vermés, G., 70
Vielhauer, P., 4, 23, 24 n, 57 n, 63, 65 n, 68, 69, 72 n, 73 n, 84 n, 85

Walker, W. O., 19, 21–22
Weeden, T. J., 78 n, 84 n, 110 n, 131
Wheelwright, P., 37–39

INDEX OF BIBLICAL REFERENCES

OLD TESTAMENT

Genesis
5:22, 24 — 29
5:24 — 28
28:12 — 16

2 Samuel
7 — 48, 56

Psalms
2:7 — 21
8 — 21
8:4 — 21
8:6 — 21, 22
16 — 20, 21
16:6 — 21
16:10 — 21
16:11 — 21
18 — 21
18:4, 5 — 21
22 — 68, 100, 101
22:7 — 77 n, 100
22:25 — 77 n
37:11 — 11
37:20 — 11

110:1 — 5, 11, 12, 13, 16, 17, 21, 22, 34, 35, 48, 55, 58, 59, 60 n, 66
118 — 76, 86, 100
118:22 — 77, 100

Isaiah
53 — 76, 77, 87, 97, 98, 99, 100, 101, 102, 103
53:3 — 77 n, 100
60:19, 20 — 30

Jeremiah
30:21 — 33

Ezekiel
1 — 28, 31
2:1 — 29

Daniel
7 — 3, 5, 25, 27–28, 28, 29, 30, 31,

60 n, 111 n
7:9 — 27
7:10 — 27
7:13-14 — 27, 48
7:13 — 4, 5, 11, 12, 13, 15, 16, 17, 21, 24, 25, 29, 30, 32, 33, 34, 35, 48, 55, 58, 59, 60 n, 66
7:14 — 30
7:27 — 27

Micah
1:6 — 11

Zephaniah
3:15-17 — 30
9:9 — 33
12:10 ff. — 5, 11, 12, 13, 14, 15, 16, 17, 18, 34, 35, 59, 60 n, 66

NEW TESTAMENT

Matthew
4:12 — 99
5:19 — 63 n
5:20 — 67
6:14-15 — 63 n
7:34 — 70
8:5-13 (= Luke

7:1-10) — 88
8:9 (= Luke 7:8) — 88, 117
8:30 — 67
10:4 — 94
10:23 — 61, 62
10:32-33 — 61, 63 n

10:32 (= Luke 9:26) — 124
11:19 (= Luke 7:34) — 67, 70, 88
11:25-27 — 56
12:32 (= Luke

145

12:10) — 52, 67, 88

13:37 — 73, 81, 91, 102

19:11 — 119

19:28 — 61, 62

24:27 — 61

24:30 — 14, 15, 35

24:37 — 61

24:44 — 61, 65

26:2 — 95

28:18 — 74, 88 n

Mark

1:1 — 114, 115

1:11 — 85, 115

1:14 — 80

1:16-3:6 — 80, 88, 117

2:1-3:6 — 80, 88

2:10 — 67, 69, 70, 74, 79, 81, 83, 85, 87, 88, 89, 112, 115–121, 124, 128

2:28 — 67, 69, 70, 74, 79, 81, 85, 88, 89, 115–121

3:6 — 80, 81, 89

3:7-6:6a — 117

3:7-12 — 112

3:11 — 115, 117

3:28-29 —72a

4:24 — 63 n

4:35-5:43 — 112

5:7 — 115, 117

6:31-52 — 112

6:53-56 — 112

8:27-10:52 — 81, 82, 90, 100, 129

8:27-10:45 — 111, 117, 118

8:27-9:1 — 109

8:27 — 90, 130

8:29 — 109, 114, 131

8:31-9:1 — 110

8:31 ff. — 109 n

8:31 — 75, 77, 81, 89, 90, 95, 100, 109, 115–121

8:34-9:1 — 109 n

8:34 ff. — 91

8:38 — 35, 61, 63, 81, 85, 89, 130

9:1 — 62, 131

9:7 — 85, 115

9:9 — 115–121

9:12 — 77, 86, 87, 95, 100, 115–121

9:12b — 79

9:30-37 — 110

9:30 — 90

9:31 ff. — 109 n

9:31 — 75, 90, 95, 100, 115–121

9:35 ff. — 91

9:41 — 114

10:1 — 90

10:32-45 — 110

10:32 ff. — 109 n

10:33-34 — 75, 90, 100

10:33 — 95, 115–121

10:38 ff. — 91

10:42-45 — 119

10:45 — 7, 67, 69, 73, 77, 79, 81, 82, 83, 87, 91, 95, 96, 97, 98, 101, 102, 103, 111 n, 115–121, 129, 130

12:10-11 — 77

12:35-37 — 13

12:35 — 114

12:36 — 22, 59

13 — 11, 131

13:1-5a — 131

13:5b-27 — 131

13:9 — 131

13:14 — 116a

13:21 — 114

13:26 — 12, 15, 16, 17, 35, 59, 60, 61, 62, 79, 82, 86, 115–121, 130, 131, 132

13:28-37 — 131

13:30 — 62

13:35-36 — 65

13:40-41 — 64 n

14:21 — 76, 79, 82, 86, 87, 101, 111 n, 115–121, 130, 131, 132

14:24 — 96, 119

14:32, 35, 40 — 77

14:41 — 76, 79, 82, 86, 87, 95, 101, 115–121, 130, 131–132, 132

14:42 — 77, 95

14:53-71 — 108

14:54, 66 — 108

14:55-65 — 108

14:61-62 — 85

14:61 — 108, 109, 114, 115

14:62 — 5, 10–21, 35, 42, 43, 59, 60, 79, 82, 86, 87, 108, 109, 115–121, 127–128, 128, 130, 132

15:32 — 114

15:39 — 85, 115

16:8 — 106

Luke

6:22 — 73

6:25 — 67

7:34 (= Matt 11:19) — 67, 69, 71

9:58 (= Matt 8:20) — 67, 69, 72

10:10 — 91

10:21-22 — 56

11:30 (= Matt

12:40) — 35, 61, 64
12:5 — 74, 88 n
12:8-9 (= Matt 10:32-33) — 35, 59, 61, 63 n, 64 n, 89, 117
12:8 (= Matt 10:32) — 64 n
12:10 (= Matt 12:32) — 67, 69, 71
12:40 (= Matt 24:44) — 61, 64 n, 65
17:23-24 (= Matt 24:26-27) — 35
17:24 (= Matt 24:27) — 61, 64
17:26-27 (= Matt 24:37-39) — 35
17:26 (= Matt 24:37) — 61, 64
17:28-30 — 61, 64
17:28 — 64 n
17:30 (= Matt 24:39) — 64
19:10 — 73, 81, 102, 119
21:27 — 15
22:24-27 — 119
22:27 — 91, 102, 118, 119
22:69 — 18
24:7 — 95

John
1:1-11 — 126–127
1:34 — 123
1:49 — 123
1:51 — 12, 15, 123, 127–128
3:13 — 123
3:14 — 64 n, 123
3:17 — 127
3:18 — 124
5:19-24 — 124

5:21 — 64 n
5:25-27 — 127
5:25 — 124, 127
5:26 — 64 n
5:27 — 123, 124, 128
6:27 — 123
6:53-54 — 124
6:53 — 123
6:62 — 123
8:28 — 123
9:35 — 123
10:31 — 127
10:36 — 124
11:4 — 124
11:27 — 124
12:23 — 123
12:34 — 123
12:50 — 64 n
13:31 — 123
14:31 — 123
17:1 — 124, 127
17:5 — 127
19:7 — 124
19:36 — 35
19:37 — 12, 14, 15, 35
20:31 — 124

Acts of the Apostles
1:9 — 12, 13, 16, 17
2:24-29 — 20
2:24 — 21
2:32 — 59
2:34 — 12
3:13 — 95
4:11 — 77, 100
7:55-56 — 12, 13, 16, 17, 34

Romans
4:25 — 76, 87, 95, 96, 97, 98, 101, 102
5:19 — 64 n
8:3-4 — 103
8:32 — 76, 87, 95, 97, 101, 103
8:34 — 13

1 Corinthians
3:17 — 63 n
11:23 — 95, 96, 99
11:24 — 96
14:38 — 63 n
15:3 — 96
15:22, 49 — 64 n
16:22 — 63 n

Galatians
1:4 — 95, 101, 103
1:9 — 63 n
2:20 — 76, 87, 95, 101, 103
4:4-5 — 103

Ephesians
1:20 — 13
5:2 — 76, 96, 101, 103
5:25 — 96, 101, 103

Colossians
3:1 — 13

Philippians
2:6-11 — 125

1 Thessalonians
1:10 — 111 n
4:16-17 — 62
5:3, 4 — 65

2 Thessalonians
2:8 — 62

1 Timothy
2:5 — 111 n
2:6 — 95, 96, 97, 98, 101, 102
3:16 — 125

Titus
2:14 — 95, 96, 97, 98, 101, 102

Hebrews
10:2 — 59

1 Peter
3:18-22 — 125, 126
3:21-22 — 13

2 Peter
3:10 — 65

1 John
2:28 — 62

Jude
14 — 19

Revelation
1:7 — 12, 13, 14, 15,
16, 17, 34–35, 35
1:10 — 59 n
3:3 — 65
3:3, 5 — 59 n
7 — 27
16:15 — 65
22:18, 19 — 63 n

INDEX OF REFERENCES TO THE APOCRYPHA

4 Ezra (2 Esdras)
Book as a whole — 5,
    25, 26, 31–32, 33

13 — 24, 25, 31–32,
    34
13:3 — 25

13:12, 25, 26, 32,
    51 — 25

INDEX OF REFERENCES TO EXTRA CANONICAL JEWISH APOCALYPTIC LITERATURE

Psalms of Solomon
17 — 25, 26, 31, 32

1 Enoch (Ethiopic

Enoch)
Book as a whole —
    26, 28–31, 33,
    60 n

37-71 (the
    Similitudes) —
    3–4, 5, 24
70, 71 — 25, 68